ESL Writers

ESL
Writers

A GUIDE FOR WRITING CENTER TUTORS

EDITED BY **Shanti Bruce & Ben Rafoth**

FOREWORD BY **Ilona Leki**

Boynton/Cook Publishers
Heinemann
Portsmouth, NH

Boynton/Cook Publishers, Inc.
A subsidiary of Reed Elsevier Inc.
361 Hanover Street
Portsmouth, NH 03801–3912
www.boyntoncook.com

Offices and agents throughout the world

Library of Congress Cataloging-in-Publication Data
    ESL Writers : a guide for writing center tutors / edited by Shanti Bruce and Ben Rafoth ; foreword by Ilona Leki.
        p. cm.
    Includes bibliographical references and index.
    ISBN 0-86709-580-6 (alk. paper)
    1. English language—Rhetoric—Study and teaching—Handbooks, manuals, etc.
2. English language—Study and teaching—Foreign speakers—Handbooks, manuals, etc. 3. Report writing—Study and teaching (Higher)—Handbooks, manuals, etc.
4. Tutors and tutoring—Handbooks, manuals, etc. 5. Writing centers—Handbooks, manuals, etc. I. Bruce, Shanti. II. Rafoth, Bennett A.

PE1404.G84 2004
808′.042′071—dc22   2004010723

Editors: Jim Strickland and Lisa Luedeke
Production: Vicki Kasabian
Cover design: Catherine Hawkes, Cat & Mouse
Typesetter: Techbooks
Manufacturing: Steve Bernier

Printed in the United States of America on acid-free paper
08   07   VP   3   4   5

We would like to acknowledge the tutors and ESL students who inspired this project and generously shared their experiences with us. Thanks to the contributors for their dedicated work and to Nancy Hayward and Kevin Dvorak for support along the way.

Contents

Part I   Cultural Contexts

A tutoring session is never limited to the student's text. Instead, it extends into the cultures of the tutor, the writer, and the institution, often revealing new values and perspectives. Examining cultural differences will help tutors understand the students they are helping and will go a long way toward bridging cultural divides.

Tutors often underestimate the enormous challenge of learning a second language. A deeper look into language learning offers insights into the ways in which ESL writers grow into their new language.

Part II   The ESL Tutoring Session

To ensure a positive outcome for the tutoring session, a good start is essential. By setting goals collaboratively and representing them visually, tutor and tutee can decide on the best way to spend their time together and keep focused on the writer's top priorities.

Knowing how to read the paper an ESL writer brings to the writing center may be the most important part of the session. What are some of various ways to read an ESL writer's paper, and how does a tutor know which one is right for the session?

When there is a disparity between what native speakers know about their language and what nonnative speakers seek to learn, it is easy for writing tutors to exert too much control over a paper. Helping tutors to find the right balance between being helpful and assuming helplessness is the focus of this chapter.

When a tutor struggles to understand an ESL writer's text, it is tempting to leap to conclusions about the meaning an ESL writer intends to convey. This chapter helps tutors avoid this pitfall.

Understanding the relationship of all the parts of a paper is just as vital in ESL writing as it is in L1 writing. This chapter helps tutors to see how they can move beyond word- and sentence-level concerns to talking about the ideas and organization of the entire paper.

ESL writers often want to know the rule behind every correction they need to make in their papers. Tutors, meanwhile, often don't know the rule or can't verbalize it. This chapter helps tutors discover how to deal with aspects of word- and sentence-level errors that frustrate ESL writers and seem unexplainable to native speakers.

When tutoring shifts from in-house to online, writers and tutors have to adjust their expectations. In this chapter, we learn from one director's experience with tutoring ESL writers in an online environment.

Avoiding plagiarism is a lesson that most tutors have rehearsed many times. Some ESL writers come from cultures that do not share our taboo against "stolen ideas" or "lifted words," however. This chapter helps tutors to understand how American academic rules for documenting sources compare to other cultures' and offers ideas for how to talk with ESL writers about problems of plagiarism.

ESL writers' needs often extend far beyond the paper they bring to a session, including interpreting a textbook, deciphering a syllabus, figuring out a professor's expectations, and editing a master's thesis. How are tutors to address needs that go beyond writing?

Promoting creative writing with ESL writers is a good way to help them broaden their experiences beyond the narrow limits of academic discourse—and have fun at the same time. This chapter shows how tutors can make their workplace a creative writing center for ESL students.

Part III   A Broader View

Have you ever wondered what ESL students' experience with tutors in their own country has been like? What can U.S. tutors learn from their counterparts in other countries? Explore these and other questions with someone who has worked in writing centers in both the United States and abroad.

It's a great language, but not an easy one to master, or to explain. Understanding just a fraction of what makes English challenging to learn will give tutors a new appreciation for the linguistic obstacles ESL students face.

Second language scholars can teach us a lot about assisting ESL students in the writing center, but if we stop there, we will have gotten only half the story. There is much to be learned from talking directly with ESL writers about their personal experiences in writing centers.

Foreword

In theory, fifteen minutes or a half an hour spent working privately with a knowledgeable tutor on a real text of the writer's choosing, for a real purpose, should be enormously helpful to a second language (L2) writer. Sounds ideal. Yet stories abound of tutor disinclination to work with L2 writers because these writers do not fit the profile of the students the tutor was trained to help; their differing needs and expectations have made tutors feel incompetent and sometimes even annoyed. L2 writers have their share of complaints as well: tutors who seem to know nothing about the structures of English that the writer seeks help with; tutors who seem to insist on dealing with nebulously broad issues of organization or development; tutors who seem to refuse to give the kind of help that writers feel they need. What should be an ideal encounter for helping L2 writers move forward with their writing morphs into frustration for both tutors and writers.

ESL Writers: A Guide for Writing Center Tutors is the first book-length attempt to address the issue of how the promise of the writing center might be better realized for L2 students. To give the greatest good, this book must generalize perhaps unavoidably about students, cultures, language acquisition, and their intersection with writing and the writing center. Nevertheless, it is crucial to keep in mind that, just as writing center tutors vary widely in their abilities, outlooks, and backgrounds, so do L2 writers, probably more widely in fact than tutors, coming as they do from such disparate educational, social, political, and economic contexts. And yet, the range of writing center precepts and techniques that is likely to serve one is likely to serve most. This volume lays out that range in chapters both accessible and sympathetic to tutors and L2 writers alike.

Contributors offer practical advice against a background of attempts to understand and explain L2 writing on its own terms. They work to help readers recognize that getting to know L2 students and a bit about their current abilities through talk not only may help tutors to direct appropriate questions or suggestions but the interaction itself may help L2 writers to further solidify aspects of English that are only hazily grasped or tentatively forming as part of their understanding of English. They urge readers to realize the novelty of the writing center experience for some L2 students and the importance of making them feel at ease by cooperating with them, exploring expectations the students bring, and setting goals flexibly and collaboratively rather than mindlessly applying writing center dogma.

While perhaps not everyone will agree with the culture-based explanations or even with all the tutoring advice offered, my hope is that this book will allow its audience of tutors—especially those with little experience of L2 writing—to find a way into more fruitful and satisfying writing center interactions with L2 writers.

Ilona Leki
Professor of English and Director of ESL
University of Tennessee

Introduction

ESL Writers is a book for peer tutors working in a campus writing center who assist college students learning to write in English as a second language (ESL). Tutoring ESL students is one of the most rewarding aspects of working in a writing center, but it can also be one of the most challenging. That's because a tutoring session is never limited to the student's text. Instead, it extends into the cultures of the tutor, the writer, and the institution, often revealing new values and perspectives. The goal of this book is to help tutors meet the challenge of assisting ESL writers by answering questions such as:

- Why does interaction in the writing center between people from different cultures often feel so different?
- What can tutors do in sessions with ESL writers besides point out problems with grammar and usage?
- How can conferences with ESL writers become more interactive and less one-sided?
- How far should tutors go in helping ESL writers? What are the limits?
- What do ESL students think about the assistance they receive in the writing center?

Before going any further, though, we need to define *ESL writer* For our purposes in this book, it is anyone whose native language is not English, who is visiting the United States from another country to study at a college or university, and who is in the process of learning to write (and speak) in English. While tutors assist ESL writers all over the world and in many different linguistic environments, this book assumes a U.S. context for learning and tutors who are native speakers of English. With this in mind, it is important to recognize that native speakers of English come from all over the world. People in Singapore, Nigeria, India, New Zealand, the Caribbean, and many other places learn English as their native tongue. Their variety of English may not sound like the varieties spoken in the United States, Canada, Britain, or Australia, but it is every bit English. For everyone else, English is a second or third language, and like any language, it can be a real challenge to learn. Tutors in the United States for whom English is a native language are an important part of helping others meet this challenge, and they are the readers for whom this book is written.

How Might Tutors Use This Book?

The best way to use *ESL Writers*, we believe, is to read each chapter as a follow-up to experiences such as

- a difficult or interesting tutoring session in your writing center
- an article or book you have read or discussed in a college class
- a discussion topic in a staff meeting or tutor training course

By connecting the ideas in this book to their experiences, tutors will, we hope, be able to take these ideas and adapt them to their own tutoring styles and institutional contexts. More important, they can use these ideas as a basis for consulting ESL experts—faculty, applied linguists, and especially ESL students themselves—who will guide them further in the best ways to assist ESL writers. There is plenty of room for discussion and debate with the ideas in these pages, and we encourage tutors to read the book critically and with an open mind. We also urge tutors to make the ideas in these pages a part of their casual conversations with all faculty and students as one way of promoting better understanding of the linguistic diversity on today's college campuses.

Organization of the Book

ESL Writers is organized in three parts. Part 1 (Cultural Contexts) and Part 3 (A Broader View) provide context and perspective for many of the issues that arise in Part 2 (The ESL Tutoring Session). In Part 1, tutors will see why the context for working with ESL writers can be different than working with native speakers of English, and what challenges students must deal with as they strive to become proficient in English. Part 2, the longest section of the book, focuses on the tutoring session itself—the frontline where tutors meet writers and sit down to read, write, and discuss as much as they can in the time available. The goal of Part 2 is to strike a balance between theory and practice in a way that helps peer tutors be as effective as they can with the training that they receive. In this section, tutors will find practical ideas they can take with them into their next session, as well as new perspectives on familiar routines. The chapters in Part 2 do not just give advice but offer realistic examples and scenarios designed to make tutors think and to help them try out new approaches. They also explain why some strategies work better than others and why some problems have no easy answers. In this section of the book, tutors will find ideas and suggestions for

- beginning the tutoring session
- reading an ESL writer's paper
- helping ESL writers say what they want to say
- viewing the paper as a whole

- editing line by line
- avoiding taking over the writer's paper
- tutoring online
- addressing cases of possible plagiarism
- understanding the limits of a tutor's responsibilities
- promoting creative writing

The chapters in Part 3 take up a few issues that have arisen in the staff meetings in our own writing center and during after-hours discussions. They have probably crossed your minds as well:

- What kind of experiences with writing do ESL students have in their own countries before coming to the United States?
- Are some languages harder to learn than others? What about English?
- What do ESL writers say about the help they receive in U.S. writing centers?

If your writing center is like most others in the United States, then there is an urgent need for better training of tutors to work with ESL students. *ESL Writers* can be an important part of this training because it addresses situations tutors encounter frequently when working with ESL writers and offers concrete suggestions that tutors can put into practice. It is written in a clear style that tutors will find accessible. And it challenges tutors to think beyond their own cultures and experiences in order to better assist ESL writers.

ESL Writers

1

Insights into Cultural Divides

Nancy Hayward

Writing about tutoring English as a second language (ESL) students without grounding it in a discussion of culture is like trying to sail a boat without knowledge of wind. It can't easily be done. Cultural expectations have everything to do with the success or failure of any tutoring session, just as wind velocity has everything to do with a successful sailing expedition. But these expectations are not always obvious. Most intercultural encounters in fact leave more unsaid than spoken, as shown in the following example. This scenario, while fictionalized, is based on observations of many writing center tutorials.

> Toshi bows before taking a seat in the chair indicated by the writing center tutor, Jessica. Sitting motionless, he waits until Jessica asks, "What would you like to work on today?" Toshi takes out a beginning draft of a paper he has started for a class in the MBA program, and stares at the floor while Jessica glances briefly through the two pages. When she finishes a cursory review, she smiles at Toshi, waiting for his answer. Thursdays are busy this time in the semester. There are three other students waiting for one of the two tutors working that day. Finally, sensing Jessica's mood, Toshi says in a hushed voice, "Is it OK?"

From Toshi's perspective,

- He is exhibiting polite behavior appropriate for the Japanese.
- He tries to be as deferential as possible.
- He silently waits to be addressed.
- He seeks agreement.
- He avoids eye contact.
- He is sensitive to the "other."

From Jessica's perspective,

- She looks for Toshi to say why he came to the writing center.
- She expects the student to define issues or problems.
- She is aware of keeping to a schedule.
- She is uncomfortable with silence.

While each person in this communicative situation is functioning according to his or her cultural scripts, they are missing important information about the other's scripts. Let's look behind the scenes to see what guides each person's communicative style.

It seems that people go about their daily lives assuming everyone perceives the world, indeed perceives their own sense of reality, the same. Yet research shows that people do not see eye-to-eye within the same culture much less across cultural boundaries. The fact remains that many people are unaware of the influence that culture exerts over our perceptions, our judgments, our mind-sets, our actions and interactions with others.

One of the main purposes in studying culture is to gain an appreciation for other ways of life. Before we begin to analyze culture, however, it is important to acknowledge that the concept of culture is a value-free concept. In other words, there is no "right" or "wrong" culture. What we want to accomplish is simply a better understanding of our own and other cultural beliefs and behaviors.

What Is Culture?

If you were to ask twenty people for a definition of *culture*, you would get twenty different answers. One person believes that culture is simply everything—the food, the clothing, the visual arts, the customs and beliefs. But another person defines culture more narrowly as opera and ballet. Samovar and Porter define culture as "the deposit of knowledge, experience, beliefs, values, attitudes, meanings, social hierarchies, religion, notions of time, roles, spatial relations, concepts of the universe, and material objects and possessions acquired by a group of people in the course of generations through individual and group striving."[1]

One popular notion says that culture is like an iceberg; it is only the top 10 percent that is visible, and the other 90 percent is submerged. The part we see—the customs, the clothing and food, the social customs—is only 10 percent. "Culture hides more than it reveals," Edward Hall says, "and strangely enough, what it hides, it hides most effectively from its own participants."[2] What, then, constitutes the remaining 90 percent? What is submerged? Let's consider the depth of culture's influence over the ways that people interact and talk.

Weekend or Le Weekend?

Have you ever been in a tutoring session in which your ESL student had a word in his own language that seemed to express his intended meaning better than any word the two of you could think of in English? It is often difficult to translate a word or concept from one language to another. Here is an example. You may think to yourself, "Surely everyone understands a term as basic as *weekend*." However, the connotations that surround the English word *weekend*, including such things as leisure, time off, two days, and even the concept of a week as time divided into working portions and nonworking portions, are not universal. In fact, the French adopted the English word *weekend* to fill a void in their lexicon because, culturally, they had a much looser division between work and play. They perceived time in a different way, but as the demands of modern work began to change their culture in the twentieth century, they felt they needed to call these two days something. *Le weekend* is now officially part of French dictionaries.

Anyone who has tried to translate an idea from one language to another knows universality of thought is improbable. Indeed, there are concepts, even words, that defy one-to-one translations essentially because cultures value and perceive the world differently. The Sapir Whorf Hypothesis addresses this issue. Developed in the 1930s by two noted linguists, Edward Sapir and Benjamin Lee Whorf, the hypothesis focuses on understanding culturally different thought patterns. Whorf gives this example of a race of people lacking the ability to perceive any color except blue. He says:

> The term *blue* would convey no meaning for them, their language would lack color terms, and their words denoting their various sensations of *blue* would answer to, and translate, our words *light, dark, white, black,* and so on, not our word *blue*.[3]

We may not choose to believe that language *determines* thought (known as the strong version of this hypothesis); we may simply believe that language exerts some influence over thought. However, most experts acknowledge that language and culture are somehow inextricably linked, and that the culture from which we come has much to do with our assumptions of the way things "ought to be."

Cultural Values

Growing up, we tend to accept the major values and beliefs of our families and the communities in which we live. Certain concepts become embedded in our day-to-day living. An example is the concept of *time* for most people in the United States. How many words or expressions do they have that relate to the concept of time?

Time's up!

You're *late!*

What *time* is it?

Do you have *time* to see me?

Time is money.

How much *time* do I have?

Time is precious.

Researchers looking into values clarification for different cultures have found that, in the United States, people have significantly more expressions for time-related activities than most other cultures, indicating time is an important cultural value.

Let me share an anecdote about how these types of cultural beliefs or values differ. While living in Mexico, I heard this story from a colleague, a Mexican woman of German descent. Her father had emigrated from Germany in the 1930s and helped establish a German school in Mexico. This man, an amateur naturalist, had an abiding interest in the jungles and mountains of rural Mexico, often spending vacations and weekends collecting specimens. On one expedition, he disappeared. His German friends, distraught over his disappearance, said, "We will spend every spare moment after work and on the weekends, searching for him." His Mexican friends also vowed to search for their friend, but their commitment had a different orientation. They said, "We will leave this day and keep searching for our friend until we find him." For the Germans, *time* at work or on task was the most important consideration. For the Mexicans, *time* was irrelevant. If a friend was lost, nothing mattered but the search.

What does this have to do with tutoring ESL writers? Quite a lot, in fact, for culture underpins our personal beliefs, our values, and our practices. If we are to begin to understand other cultures, we must first strive to understand our own. To start the process of cultural self-awareness, we must look at our assumptions in the following areas.[4]

Patterns of perceptions and thinking   In the United States, the form of "deep" or analytic thinking, originating in ancient Greece, emphasizes objective or analytic thinking. Contrast this with early Buddhist thought that relies on perceptions and sensations as the source of knowledge, and one can see the beginnings of culturally different thought patterns between the United States and other Westerners' cultures and such Eastern cultures as Chinese and Japanese.

Language and nonverbal behavior   The two aspects to this category, the linguistic and the nonlinguistic messages people send, receive, and comprehend, are essential components of any communicative situation. Linguistically, what one says communicates more than ideas and feelings; it also represents that person's worldview. Even the amount of language used by a speaker is culturally determined. In the United States, the verbally fluent person is considered witty or intelligent, but in some Native American populations, silence is highly valued and considered the mark of a wise person. In the same ways that languages are learned, our nonverbal messages are also learned from our cultures. In the United States, people make a circle with thumb and forefinger to signal OK, but that same gesture is considered obscene in Mexico. While it is interesting to see how people from other parts of the world use different gestures, a more important issue is how (mis)understandings of nonverbal messages can influence a tutorial, for few gestures have universal meaning including the concept of *time* previously noted.

Forms of activity   The division between the meanings of those in the United States of *work* and *play* allows to understand the English word *weekend* to its fullest extent. To put the United States' distinction between *work* and *play* into perspective, consider how modern Greek culture blurs the distinction. For instance, family members come to work with the employee or families work together in a small business, eating and socializing at the workplace much more frequently than in the United States.

Forms of social relationships   This category includes the notion of human equality, cooperation, and fair play in the United States. Other cultures have no problem labeling groups of people according to the caste in which they were born. Is one philosophy right and the other inherently wrong? Interculturalists say that no culture is superior to another; they are just different.

Perceptions of the world   This category considers how people see themselves in relation to nature. In the United States, people believe it is possible to control and master the natural world. For example, the U.S. government has created dams and tried to fight wildfires. Is this a universal approach to such natural events as heavy rains and fires? No, and as a matter of fact, interculturalists use the two cultures in the United States—mainstream or Anglo Americans and Native Americans—to point out how the government has been in conflict with Native Americans over uses of natural resources and land. Native Americans view nature as sacred, yet U.S. bureaucracy sees nature as commodity. This may also be the reason why private, individual ownership of property is highly valued in U.S. culture.

Perceptions of the self   It is especially important to consider how individuals view themselves in relation to the larger group. Most people in the United States value individuality and see themselves as loosely connected to society, able to forge their own futures and identities. Other cultures, notably many Asian cultures, see the group as the frame of reference. Students from such cultures feel constrained by societal pressures to conform to a much greater degree than U.S. students. To show the contrast, think about how each student in the United States is encouraged to do his own work and the value placed on that work. In Taiwan, however, the group is the important frame of reference; their philosophy is "the nail that sticks up is the one that gets hammered down."

As we uncover the cultural expectations, values, behaviors, and preferences of others, we also begin to understand that our own beliefs are relative and not absolute. This, then, is the beginning of cross-cultural understanding. As we look at ideas for bridging the cultural divide between ESL students and their English-speaking tutors, we realize there are many ways that culture insinuates itself in a writing tutorial.

Culture and Tutoring

In essence, culture rears its head in every tutorial where a native English-speaking tutor works with a nonnative-English-speaking writer. As a matter of fact, if we define *culture* more narrowly, we might see "culture" within any language group. In the United States, we might have the economic culture of white, middle-class students, or the culture of Hispanic students or the culture of eighteen-year-old women. First, there is the issue of how culture influences written text. Then there is the interpersonal or face-to-face dimension of tutoring that is impacted by culture. Before we begin, however, let's examine how cultures differ in the ways they conceptualize knowledge and learning.

People in the United States are often surprised to hear that many Europeans consider them shallow and poorly educated. Students in the United States have fallen behind in standardized tests across many different cultures, Europeans point out. They may ask: Why don't Americans know more of their own and world history? Why do U.S. schools and universities trivialize the importance of memorization? Isn't that the basis of all learning? Aren't end-of-the-year tests the most important way we have of judging overall knowledge and learning? These are good questions. In fact, a discussion of these points highlights just how far apart we are in defining what it means to be *well educated*. For many people in the United States, being well educated means being able to apply knowledge to a real situation. For an Italian, being well educated means being able to explicate theory and reproduce extended text. In many U.S. institutions, contemporary writers have replaced the classics, and yet Europeans consider the classics as basic to all education. The very notion of the function of the classroom is different, for much of the world, classroom is the place where one listens to lectures, and, as if to reinforce the teacher–student roles, blocks of desks are bolted to the floor. In Bulgaria, graduate students assert that they are assigned one chapter of a textbook to read a week; the function of the classroom is the place where the professor lectures on the important information from that chapter. In other words, knowledge is a top-down experience for Bulgarian students. They are confused when an American professor asks, "What do you think?" for they have not experienced a situation in which a professor or another authority figure solicited their opinions. When U.S.–trained tutors begin tutorials, they are often taught to use a standard opening like, "What would you like to work on today?" While this gives U.S. students the opportunity to verbalize their needs, it may only serve to confuse international students who expect a more directive approach.

The Cultural Roots of Written Text

Culture can have a great influence over tutors' expectations about the writing a person produces. The elements to keep in mind when tutoring a text are contrastive rhetoric, genre, and the student's level of language aquisition.

Contrastive Rhetoric

Contrastive rhetoric refers to the ways that cultures differ in their expectations about rhetorical patterns or logical organization of a text. One expert in second language writing says, "Contrastive rhetoric maintains that language and writing are cultural phenomenon. As a result, each language has rhetorical conventions unique to it."[5] In other words, U.S. students have been taught to write a five-paragraph essay, but Korean students have been taught a different way of organizing their papers. According to Robert Kaplan, the person who coined the term *contrastive rhetoric*, and based on an analysis of 600 texts written by ESL students, we can see several cultural generalizations.[6]

Many of our international students studying in the United States are Asians who have been taught in the rhetoric of their cultures. Japanese, Koreans, Taiwanese, and Thai students have told me that they approach a topic from a variety of viewpoints in order to examine it indirectly, a process that indicates, to them, careful thinking. To a U.S.–trained tutor, this might indicate lack of focus or indecisiveness. However, this circling around a topic is the polite way to proceed, for Asians see the direct approach as rude or abrupt. Unlike the Japanese or Thai, U.S. and British writers tend toward deductive reasoning where a thesis statement is located in a prominent position, usually in the first paragraph. The subsequent paragraphs develop the thesis in a linear way until the conclusion wraps it up.

Kaplan described writers of French and Spanish as having "much greater freedom to digress or to introduce extraneous material." To a U.S. tutor, this might look like writing that goes off the topic. A French-speaking African graduate student once described himself as having more freedom to invent and include information that may not be directly related to the thesis. The example he gave is this: If you're telling a story about going to the post office to mail a package, you might tell all the elements that happen along the way—the friends and neighbors you stop to talk to, the animals you see wandering around the streets, the thoughts that you had. You don't just say that you arrived and mailed the package. A Spanish-speaking Costa Rican woman shared a similar thought when she announced cheerfully, "I always write run-on sentences!" I was taken aback since the term *run-on sentence* strikes fear in

American students' hearts. This student, however, had none of the negative connotations associated with run-on sentences, as she explained that in Spanish "we tend to over explain. I can't explain things in ten words; my sentences are like thirty words long because I have thoughts that are kind of related to the topic, and that's OK in Spanish."

Arabic speakers also report that their writing is less direct than writing in English, and they have difficulty when trying to write in English. One reason for this is the Arabic sensitivity to politeness, represented by indirectness. Rather than getting to the point, native Arabic speakers might open up a topic and talk around the point. Tutors see this as including information that is not directly connected to the topic. It might also be represented by writing that makes extended use of coordination (using *and, but, or, for, nor,* etc.) within a sentence and across sentence boundaries.[7]

While Kaplan's distinction of culturally different schemata has not had universal agreement, his work is important in looking at the differing expectation readers and writers have for rhetorical structure. Paul Kei Matsuda explains: "The linguistic explanation emphasizes the prominence of the writer's L1 as an influencing—if not determining—factor in the L2 organizational structures."[8]

In the simplest terms, cultural differences may be manifested

- in a paper's organization (such as inductive or deductive reasoning patterns)
- in a preference for a particular sentence style (Spanish sentences that seem to be only loosely organized and that seem to have no boundaries that connect the sentence's development with its topic)
- in the forms of address or register (issues of formality)
- in apparent lack of cohesive ties
- in the amount or type of information that is included (In student essays written in English, for example, Bulgarian students make generalizations and write abstractly without providing specific information or concrete details, contradicting the explicit instructions from a tutor or teacher.)

Understanding contrastive rhetoric may help tutors to see how students have drafted papers that are culturally appropriate for their first language but that don't work in English. It may help both tutors and ESL students to engage in an open discussion of how each culture has rhetorical expectations. It is even a way to see how a consideration of context influences the written product.

Genre

International students sometimes have no experience with genres of writing common in the United States. It is not unusual for Europeans to have advanced degrees without ever having written an academic research-based paper.

I remember a Russian MA student who had no experience in academic writing save her undergraduate thesis. Others are uncomfortable with some genres. In particular, Japanese students may feel that personal writing is risky because it asks them to reveal more personal information—emotions, feelings, or opinions—than they are comfortable with. Another example comes from Eastern Europe: When asked to write a two-page response to a reading assignment, a Ukrainian student had no concept of what that entailed. Should he write a summary? he asked. How could he, a mere graduate student, *reflect* on what an expert had written?

Level of Language Acquisition

Avoidance phenomenon is a concept that comes from studies of second language acquisition. The idea is that students who have not yet mastered a linguistic form, concept, sentence type, grammatical unit, or vocabulary word tend to avoid types of writing that put them in the position of having to produce what they find difficult. This may mean that tutors encounter students who have written little because they don't have mastery over the language form with which to express their ideas. An example might be this: A tutor reads a student's paper narrating an experience in which the writer learns an important life lesson. The tutor feels that background information is missing from the paper and questions the student. While the student can explain the background information orally, she cannot manage the intricate verb tenses to show stages of past events. In fact, the student simply felt it was easier to leave out the information.

Tutors encounter writers, both U.S. and ESL, who make mistakes when drafting. It is generally agreed that mistakes result from lack of attention and not from incomplete knowledge. Mistakes often happen in native English-speaking students' writing as momentary lapses, as in using the word *there* instead of *their*. Mistakes also happen with ESL students when writers are not focused on the language forms; international students can demonstrate knowledge of the rule, but simply have made a mistake. Errors, on the other hand, are consistent problem areas, that indicate faulty or incomplete knowledge. In this sense, ESL students are no different from native English writers for they too make mistakes as well as errors. Being able to ascertain whether a student is making a mistake or an error will help the tutor devise strategies for the tutorial. For a full discussion of mistakes versus errors in language acquisition, see Chapter 2.

Another issue is plagiarism. Several years ago I received a paper on "The Pillars of Islam" that sounded like it had been copied from the Koran. In fact, I learned that the student had memorized the passage, and then for my assignment, simply "transcribed" it word for word. To many of the world's population, this is an acceptable—indeed commendable—way to write. Replicating the words and ideas of a great scholar or thinker shows respect and deference, and according to my Pakistani student, this was what he was doing in his paper. To me, a professor in the United States, this was clearly plagiarism. In the United States there is a strong aversion to using another person's words or ideas, and plagiarism is considered cheating. Since many cultures do not share this view, sometimes tutors must engage in a frank discussion of cultural attitudes. (For a fuller discussion of plagiarism, see Chapter 10.)

ESL writers often lack experience. While writing as a means of assessment has gained prominence in the past few years, written, discrete-knowledge or oral examinations are still *de rigeur* in most international settings. Many ESL writers have little-to-no experience with the five-paragraph essay, and an extended research paper is alien to them. Students coming to a writing center for help could have good language skills but little understanding of the role writing plays in U.S. institutions. These students need help with brainstorming, drafting, and revising, in fact, the entire writing process.

The Cultural Roots of Intercultural Communication

Nonverbal Communication

Eye contact has been identified as the most important nonverbal communicator we have at our disposal. People in the United States see direct eye contact as a signal that we are listening; Japanese show they are listening by averting their eyes. To make direct eye contact is a sign of disrespect, especially between Japanese males and females. In contrast, most Middle Easterners feel uneasy unless they can see clearly the pupils of the other's eyes. However, because the implications of eye behavior varies from culture to culture and between genders, it is difficult to make generalizations, but it is important to keep in mind that international students' lack of eye contact is not necessarily a sign of inattentiveness.

The physical distance between speakers is another strong nonverbal communicator. In the United States, most people prefer greater personal space. Research shows that North Americans as well as Northern Europeans tend to feel more comfortable if they maintain a "bubble" of about three feet of personal space. Others, Latin Americans and people from Mediterranean cultures in particular, report they like to be closer. Related to personal space is the issue of touching. Touching may be regarded as appropriate in one culture and just the opposite in another. In a study of comparative touch behavior at cafés in London and Paris, researchers noted that within the space of an hour, French couples touched each other more than one hundred times. The British couples did not touch each other at all.[9] Gesturing, too, causes some confusion. In Bulgaria, the custom is to rock the head side-to-side to indicate "yes" and shake the head up and down to indicate "no." Some tutors have reported being confused when working with students who have different or conflicting gestures from those familiar in the United States.

Vocal feedback or supportive overlapping vocalization is called *backchanneling*. Backchanneling includes such vocalizations as *yup, OK, hmmm,* and other utterances to show you are listening when another person is speaking. Japanese tend to give vocal indications they are listening much more than Americans. For those tutors who see "having the floor" as their uninterrupted time, this may seem to be rude behavior. Indeed, cultures determine what is deemed as supportive additions to a conversation and what is seen as interrupting behavior.

Issues of privacy are important during tutoring sessions because many cultures view writing as private. Some students, especially those from highly contextualized cultures, one where meaning is embedded in the context of a situation, may feel shame by being thrust into the limelight. Chinese, Japanese, and Korean students view their identity as belonging to a group; they may become uncomfortable being exposed by having their writing on display.

Finally, messages are sent nonverbally by silence. Silence is often uncomfortable for people in the United States. In many countries, the United States and Great Britain for example, verbal expertise is prized. But for many Asians, there is no such thing as a pregnant silence. For Japanese students, the feeling that "fewer words are better" is powerful. For tutors, it is important to know that most Japanese are comfortable with silence. In observations between two Japanese, silences of up to 30 minutes have been routinely documented.[10] Sheila Ramsey considers what silence means for the Japanese:

> It may have many situational meanings: time to formulate an opinion or consider the appropriate form or content of a remark; a gathering of courage to speak in English; a space while waiting for a *sempai* (senior) to speak first; or the formation of a generally less confrontational, softer way to convey a disagreement.[11]

Cultural Preferences for Interpersonal Communication

Spoken cross-cultural communication includes many components; some are important because they may directly affect tutorials with ESL students. In a general sense, the functional uses of language are defined by each culture, both in the frequency of use and in the forms they take. For instance, many international students are confused by invitations. When a U.S. student says, "We'll have to get together soon," the international student may believe a concrete invitation has been extended and is disappointed when in fact there is none. From the U.S. perspective, "We'll have to get together soon" is simply a way of closing a conversation. A Malaysian student related another example. As she walked on campus, a stranger made eye contact and said, "How ya doin'?" to which the Malaysian began to tell of her problems in course registration. Finally, she realized "How ya doin'?" was simply a greeting and not a request for information. Like these previous examples, the following issues have a direct effect on interactions during a tutorial session.

First is the issue of directness versus indirectness. The United States is a country where directness, *telling it like it is* or *laying it all out on the table*, is valued. Other cultures might find this approach blunt and offensive.[12] One Indonesian student asked me, "Will I ever learn how to say things directly like an American?" for she was struggling to fit in to U.S. culture. When tutors work with international students from a culture that values indirectness such as Asian or Arabic cultures, they should understand that one culture's openness is another's rudeness.

Another issue related to directness is the concept of cooperation versus individuality. In some cultures, like in the United States and Germany, individual rights and expectations are valued. In cultures such as these, individuals are expected to voice their needs, expectations, and opinions. However, in other cultures, individuals seek harmony with the group, and in order to maintain harmony, they defer to the authority. This is often the case with Japanese, Chinese, Korean, and Thai students. In a writing center, such deferential behavior might be manifested as agreement with the tutor or subjugation of a student's preferences for written expression. On the other hand, I have noticed that many Eastern Europeans, Bulgarians in particular, tend to be extremely direct and to challenge others' ideas and thoughts. People in the United States can and often do find these ways of voicing opinions offensive.

Politeness and formality are cultural variables. Hispanic, Asian, Middle Eastern, and other cultures with a hierarchical social stratification find egalitarian informality in the United States to be shocking. Yet people in the United States find these cultures to be overly polite and solicitous. Tutors who find themselves uncomfortable in a formal situation might find a way of communicating that provides a less formal environment, especially in tutoring situations.

Each culture defines what it means to be masculine and feminine. In addition, there may be taboos about males and females working in close proximity to each other. In a tutorial, there may be some concerns about a male tutee working with a female tutor or a female tutee working with a male tutor.

Psychological and Social Aspects

As with the other categories, there are individual differences when we look at psychological and social components of interaction. One of the most important is anxiety because of power relationships.

- International students might be anxious in a writing center because it is a new environment.
- Many ESL students come from cultures where teachers are venerated and followed without question, and the teacher–student relationship in such a culture is fraught with tensions.

Another source of anxiety comes from the tutorial itself.

• Tutors might be regarded as figures of power. Some international students are anxious to please teachers or tutors; they tend to rely on input from experts. This may frustrate tutors who try to get writers to take ownership for their own ideas and writing.

• On the other hand, some ESL students may distrust younger tutors, feeling they do not have the experience and authority of older, more experienced tutors.

Just as with any group of U.S. students, we find ESL students who are experienced in writing and are confident and those who lack experience and confidence.

Many ESL writers are unable to get their points across. This often happens when students believe everyone feels or believes exactly as they do. Some ESL students come from homogeneous, high-context cultures whose members tend to share a worldview. In Bulgaria, a country that is just emerging from relative isolation, 90 percent of the population is Bulgar. Bulgarians tend to have remarkably similar worldviews; their shared history and stable, homogeneous population has given them little chance for interacting with people outside of the region. In turn, this leads Bulgarian students to assume everyone believes as they do and to make general assertions about these beliefs. However, the United States is a heterogeneous nation and much of our intended meaning must be negotiated. An example might be that a tutor may need to explain the difference between reader-based writing and writer-based writing to clarify the issue for these students.

International students have different beliefs about accepting or demanding help. In some cultures, accepting help can been seen as a weakness. In fact, I was surprised to learn that an Arabic-speaking male student had not visited the writing center as I had requested. I found that he felt it was shameful to admit weakness. Even though he knew he needed help with his writing, this student chose to seek advice from within the Arabic community (see Chapter 15 for more about this issue). Other cultures may view tutors as paid workers, employed only to serve students. A writing center tutor told this story as an example. As she was walking across campus, an international student stopped her to ask for help on his paper. When the tutor said that she was not currently working, he was confused. Wasn't she a tutor? he asked. From his perspective, a tutor is always a tutor no matter what the context. From this U.S. tutor's perspective, time off duty meant time off limits.

Tutoring ESL writers is both demanding and enlightening. While there are cultural profiles and national characteristics, it is important to remember that each student is an individual with unique needs and talents. In a sense, each time an ESL student comes into the writing center, the tutor is presented with a cultural puzzle for which there is no easy solution. The following checklist is intended to help each tutor begin thinking about tutorials with ESL students.

Checklist or Questionnaire for Tutors

- What do I know about this student's cultural background?
- What do I know about this student's linguistic background and linguistic assumptions?
- Does this paper reveal mainly a language problem or a writing problem?
- For whom is this paper intended? Is it for an English class?
- Should I be directive or nondirective in dealing with this student? For how long?
- What patterns of error do I see?
- Can I distinguish between the meta-issues that are cultural and the local issues that are a result of language acquisition?
- Is it OK to teach grammar or vocabulary to this student?

Learning about other cultures can be an exciting adventure, one that begins by learning about our own cultural expectations. As we enter this globalized era, we realize the need for deeper understandings of other people and ourselves. Remember this is as important in the writing center as it is in politics, government, education, and business. Enjoy your journey.

Notes

1. Samovar and Porter, 7.
2. Hall (1998), 59.
3. Whorf, 87.
4. These categories are established by Stewart and Bennett (1991).
5. Ferris and Hedgcock, 11.
6. Kaplan, 18.
7. Kaplan, 15.
8. Matsuda, 243.
9. Gesteland (2003).
10. Ramsey, 120.
11. Ramsey, 120.
12. Stewart and Bennett, 156.

Works Cited

Ferris, Dana, and John S. Hedgcock. 1998. *Teaching ESL Composition: Purpose, Process and Practice*. Mahwah, NJ: Lawrence Erlbaum.

Gesteland, Richard R. "Spanning the Chasm of Culture Gap." General Management Review [cited 28 July 2003]; available from www.etgmr.com/gmrjan-mar3/art3.html.

Hall, Edward T. 1992. *An Anthropology of Everyday Life*. New York: Doubleday.

———. 1998. "The Power of Hidden Differences." In *Basic Concepts in Intercultural Communication*, edited by Milton J. Bennett, 53–68. Yarmouth, ME: Intercultural Press.

Hudson, R. A. 1999. *Sociolinguistics*. 2d ed. Cambridge: Cambridge University Press.

Kaplan, Robert. B. 2001. "Cultural Thought Patterns in Inter-Cultural Education." In *Landmark Essays on ESL Writing*, edited by Tony Silva and Paul Kei Matsuda, 11–25. Mahwah, NJ: Lawrence Erlbaum.

Matsuda, Paul Kei. 2001. "Contrastive Rhetoric in Context: A Dynamic Model of L2 Writing." In *Landmark Essays on ESL Writing*, edited by Tony Silva and Paul Kei Matsuda, 241–55. Mahwah, NJ: Lawrence Erlbaum.

Ramscy, Sheila J. 1998. "Interactions between North Americans and Japanese: Considerations of Communication Style." In *Basic Concepts of Intercultural Communication*, edited by Milton J. Bennett, 111–30. Yarmouth, ME: Intercultural Press.

Samovar, Larry A., and Richard E. Porter. 2000. "Understanding Intercultural Communication: An Introduction and Overview." In *Intercultural Communication*, edited by Larry A. Samovar and Richard E. Porter, 5–16. Boston: Wadsworth.

Stewart, Edward C., and Milton J. Bennett. 1991. *American Cultural Patterns*. Yarmouth, ME: Intercultural Press.

Whorf, Benjamin Lee. 1998. "Science and Linguistics." In *Basic Concepts in Intercultural Communication*, edited by Milton J. Bennett, 85–95. Yarmouth, ME: Intercultural Press.

2

Theoretical Perspectives on Learning a Second Language

Theresa Jiinling Tseng*

While trying to help English as a second language (ESL) students in your writing center, you may have wondered, Why do ESL writers seem to have trouble getting the correct word order? Why do ESL writers need help choosing the right word? Why do they continue to make the same errors time after time? Is there anything teachers or tutors can do to make learning English any easier for ESL students? These are also some of the same questions that drive research in the field known as second language acquisition (SLA), a part of the discipline of applied linguistics. While second language scholars have not settled the answers to these questions, their theories have provided important background knowledge to help explain the challenges of learning a second language.

I have organized this chapter around four of the major approaches to theories of second language acquisition, and by presenting them in a way that I hope is easy to understand, I believe you will be able to grasp their major concepts. They will shed light on the discipline of SLA and bring you closer to understanding those students who are writing in English as their second (or third or fourth) language.

Presented in chronological order, the theories may be described as (1) Behaviorist, (2) Innatist, (3) Cognitivist, and (4) Interactionist.[1] This chapter introduces you to these theories and illustrates how they can apply to ESL writers in the context of a tutorial. It is my hope that this knowledge will not only make you a more informed tutor, but also one who is also more curious about, engaged in, and empathetic to the challenges ESL writers face.

* I am grateful to John Dunn for his constructive feedback on an earlier version of this chapter.

Behaviorist—You Learn by Drill and Practice

Anyone who has ever had to recite multiplication tables or memorize lines for a play knows that repetition can be a helpful strategy for learning new material. When this repetition becomes so automatic that you no longer have to think about it, you have formed a habit. This habit formation is one way to account for second language (L2) learning. In this view, language learning involves:

- receiving input (exposure to the new language),
- imitating and practicing it repeatedly (drill),
- getting encouragement (positive reinforcement) for doing it correctly, and
- eventually, forming associations between words and objects or events.

For example, to use the expression "bless you" correctly, an L2 learner goes through

1. receiving input (someone teaches her, "Say 'bless you' when you see someone sneezing" or she sees a person say "bless you" when someone sneezes),
2. practicing "Bless you" whenever she sees someone sneezing,
3. receiving "Thank you" in response, and
4. after many practices, eventually establishing the habit of saying "Bless you" when someone sneezes.

In language teaching, practices such as sentence drills and memorization of sentence patterns are often used to form and strengthen the habit of using the new language correctly. Tutors, and other native speakers, often use similar drill-and-practice exercises in foreign language classes of their own to establish the new language habits, and errors are corrected immediately so that bad habits will not be developed.

Applying the behaviorist view to SLA, we assume that the language habits of L2 learners' first language (L1) influence their learning of the second language. This assumption is called the Contrastive Analysis Hypothesis (CAH), and it states that learners have an easier time learning a second language when it is structurally similar to their first language, and they have a more difficult time when the two are substantially different.[2] Here is a conversation between a tutor, Joe, and an L2 learner, Maria, about an error caused by the influence of Maria's L1, which is Spanish:

Joe: Maria, why did you say "I received a pair of *shoes news* for my birthday"?

Maria: Look (pointing to her shoes), they are *news*.

Joe: Oh, you mean they are your *new shoes*.

Maria: Why can't I say *shoes news*? In Spanish, we say, "zapatos nuevos" (shoes news).

Joe: In English, we put the description (the adjective) before the thing
          (the noun) we describe. So, *new* goes before *shoes*. And, we don't
          make the adjective plural even though the noun might be plural.

The error in this example is known as a *transfer error* because Maria followed two Spanish grammar rules that do not transfer to writing in English: (1)
nouns go before adjectives in word order, and (2) adjectives must match nouns in
singularity/plurality. Tutors could help Maria by pointing out the error to her. At
this point, you may wonder why it is necessary to point out the error instead of
letting her discover it herself. Errors caused by the interference from learners first
language are difficult, and sometimes impossible, for them to figure out without
help. In the example, Maria felt that she was correct because she followed familiar Spanish grammar rules. Without explicit correction, Maria's meaning gets dis-
torted because *news* is not the plural form of *new,* as Maria had imagined. When
tutors notice that the errors are caused by the L2 learner's mother tongue, and the
errors remain unchanged after the learner's self-editing, tutors should not hesitate
to point them out because the L2 learner often appreciates tutors who correct
transfer errors he could not detect by himself. Unless tutors know their student's
native language, however, they will not be able to recognize specific transfer
errors. Some knowledge of the student's first language may help.

Like most theories, the CAH does not tell the whole story of second language learning. For example, it cannot identify all of the errors that students
need to correct. It also predicts many errors that do not occur, and it cannot
account for learners who avoid using structures with which they are not familiar. In sum, it may be that the CAH gives us a snapshot of part of the theoretical landscape rather than the entire view.

Innatist—You Are Hardwired to Learn a Language

Another way to account for an L2 learner's language development is related to
an idea about L1 learning proposed by the well-known linguist Noam Chomsky: All young children are hardwired to learn their L1.[3] While some linguists
believe that this innate ability is not available for L2 learners past puberty, others say that it may still be available because people who learn a new language
create many sentences they have never heard before. Some linguists believe
that L2 learners' language learning ability must be different from the L1 learners' because L2 learners have already learned one language.

Chomsky drew an important distinction in his theory of language learning—the distinction between *competence* and *performance. Competence* refers
to one's knowledge of the language, and *performance* refers to the use of that
language. A native speaker's competence develops naturally and is manifested
as his intuitions for judging whether the performance (the use of language)
is grammatical (as a native speaker would say it). A nonnative speaker's
competence of the target L2 (the language she is trying to learn), on the other

hand, does not develop completely naturally. Most L2 learners do not grow up with or acquire their L2 target but take classes to learn it. As a result, their competence often takes the form not of intuition but of knowledge of the grammar rules that they have learned. They rely on these rules to judge whether or not something is grammatical. Here's an example that illustrates how a tutor, Tina, and an advanced L2 learner, Ling, judge grammaticality:

Ling: (Reading aloud) . . . so my teacher gave me an advice.

Tina: An advice? That doesn't sound right.

Ling: Why not? The word *advice* begins with a vowel, so I used *an* before *advice.*

Tina: But we don't say "an advice."

Ling: What about "some advices"? Can I use the plural form?

Tina: Hmm, we don't say "some advices" either. We say, "some advice."

Ling: Why? Why can't we use the plural form?

The article system (a/an/the) in English often presents problems for learners whose L1 does not have articles (such as Chinese or Japanese). The usage of articles may often depend on a tacit sense (the native speaker's intuition) of discourse, Buell explains.[4] This intuition for the English article system is what Ling does not have. Ling, an advanced L2 learner whose L1 is Chinese, carefully added *an* before *advice* only to be told she made an error. In fact, Ling's problem was caused by another sense that differs from the native speaker's: the distinction between count and noncount nouns. To Ling, *advice* was countable, so she used the article *an* at first, and her attempt to change *an advice* to *some advices* still resulted in an error because *advice* is considered to be a noncount noun in English. Tina, the native-English-speaking tutor, could tell by intuition that it was not grammatical because it did not sound right. In addition, the example also shows that Ling depended heavily on her knowledge of grammar rules to reason through the usage. The point here is that grammar rules cannot possibly tell the learner everything she needs to know in order to produce error-free sentences because there are some aspects of language production that depend upon L1 intuition.

In fact, there are many instances that cannot be explained by learning the rules in grammar books. For example, we say that people eat *rice* (always in singular form) versus *beans* (always in plural form); people are *in* the car but *on* the bus, and people *watch* TV but *see* a movie. When a tutor is asked why the choice is this but not that, he will usually reply, "It just is" (see Rafoth, Chapter 14). For idiomatic expressions and usages that cannot be explained by grammar rules but only by the native English-speaking (NES) tutor's intuition, the best way to help the learner is simply to tell her, "This is what a native speaker would use intuitively."

Applying Chomsky's distinction between competence and performance, Stephen Pit Corder relates *error* to failure in *competence* (wrong knowledge or lack of knowledge), and *mistakes* to failure in *performance* (e.g., a slip of the tongue or typos).[5] A tutor cannot always tell whether the deviant sentences she sees are errors or mistakes; nonetheless, if she notices that the same problem appears repeatedly even after the L2 learner has proofread, then there is a good chance that the learner's knowledge of the usage is incorrect. In other words, it may be an error or competence problem. In addition to L1 transfer errors (involving, for example, prepositions, article usages, and word order), errors caused by L2 learners' insufficient or incorrect knowledge are also the ones learners cannot detect by themselves. This is true no matter how many times they read their writing aloud. If the learners are motivated to learn, tutors should not hesitate to point out those errors explicitly.

A Model Related to the Innatist View: Krashen's Monitor Model

Young children's acquisition of their first language is a feat that adult L2 learners cannot help but admire. Stephen Krashen, one of the most influential applied linguists, proposed to re-create the naturalist language acquisition experience of young children for second language learners.[6] His Monitor Model of second language acquisition, a model related to the innatist view, consists of five key ideas:

1.   the acquisition/learning hypothesis

2.   the monitor hypothesis

3.   the natural order hypothesis

4.   the comprehensible input hypothesis

5.   the affective filter hypothesis

For tutors interested in how people learn a second language, the Monitor Model is a useful guide.

The Acquisition/Learning Hypothesis

Acquiring a language is different from learning one. *Acquisition* refers to the process of picking up a language the way young children do—subconsciously. Krashen believes that the best way for the L2 learner to become competent in another language is by acquisition, or exposure to the L2 input at a level the learner understands while the learner's attention is on meaning and not on grammar. *Learning*, on the other hand, is consciously studying the language (the grammar rules). In Krashen's view, learned competence does not become acquired competence, so he denies a role for conscious learning in language acquisition.[7] Also, Krashen indicates that acquisition, but not learning, is responsible for fluency. This is so because formal learning makes the learners conscious of grammar rules. Consequently, the learners tend to inspect or monitor their grammar, and hence reduce the fluency, in their speech and writing. The inspection may reduce their fluency and make their speech and writing seem halting.

Krashen's Learning/Acquisition Hypothesis can explain the differences in writing difficulties between immigrant and international ESL students. For example, an immigrant student of mine wrote *firstable* instead of *first of all* to state his first point. He understood the meaning and he knew how to use the expression, yet the form was incorrect. Apparently this student had acquired, or picked up the use of the expression, but he had not acquired the form. Joy Reid points out that immigrant students often acquire with their ears many English expressions from the environment without formally learning about them.[8] Immigrant students may be relatively fluent in speaking, but they may have limited understanding of the structures of the English language. Similar to L1 students' errors, many immigrant ESL students' errors are caused by the differences between speaking and writing. For this reason, oral fluency does not always go hand-in-hand with grammatical accuracy, and oral proficiency is not necessarily related to writing proficiency. Though immigrant students may have more intuitive sense than international students of what sounds right, they may need to explicitly learn some grammar rules when their acquisition-by-ear has misled them. (See Chapters 4 and 15.)

Many international students, by contrast, have learned English by studying vocabulary and grammar rules. They often understand and can explain grammar, yet they lack the experience of hearing and using English in daily life. Their word choice and sentence structures are often unconventional. "I don't know how to express my meaning in English" is often their complaint. The point is that international students lack nativelike intuitions about what sounds right on paper. They need corrections that are pointed out explicitly for the problems that they cannot fall back on their own intuitions to fix. As Rafoth (Chapter 14) points out, this is a good reason for tutors to study the structure of English grammar.

The Monitor Hypothesis: The Spotlight

Monitoring is like examining each word or structure in the grammar spotlight. Krashen argues that Monitor operates when time allows, when correctness matters, and when the learner knows the rules. It is easier to employ Monitor in writing than in spontaneous conversation since writing allows more time to focus on form. Therefore, when L2 writers focus on meaning, their Monitors are very likely not fully operating; consequently they often forget about inflections (e.g., -s or -ed endings) when they talk or write in a hurry, or even when they are too relaxed, not paying enough attention to the inflections. In other words—and this is an important point for tutors to remember—it appears to be difficult to have fluency and accuracy at the same time. Since monitoring is like editing, an appropriate amount of monitoring is necessary to achieve accuracy. However, overmonitoring may cause writer's block, which is something many ESL students have experienced in the process of writing when they worry too much about grammatical accuracy.

The Natural Order Hypothesis: Similar Order in L1 and L2 Acquisition

Krashen's Natural Order Hypothesis states that both L1 and L2 learners follow a similar order in acquiring certain morphemes (grammatical structures such as *-ing, -s,* or articles) and make similar mistakes in the developmental processes. For example, at a stage of their language development, some young children and adult L2 learners may overgeneralize (overuse) the past tense *-ed* and use *goed* for the past tense of *go.* Tutors need to be patient with morpheme errors such as third personal singular (*-s*) and plural noun (*-s*) because they often add no meaning to communication and hence are very difficult for L2 writers to acquire.

The Comprehensible Input Hypothesis: Understanding Leads to Acquisition

The Comprehensible Input Hypothesis predicts that for L2 learners to move from one stage to the next, they need to be exposed to L2 input (the new language) that is a little bit beyond their current level but easy enough to understand. The context sometimes helps the learner understand the new language. For example, an L2 learner may understand the word *chilly* when someone is shivering and saying, "It's chilly today." Input can also become comprehensible to the learner when native speakers use so-called *foreigner talk,* which is characterized by a slower rate of speech, repetition, or paraphrasing. When tutoring, tutors may want to paraphrase certain difficult words or make use of gestures or contextual clues to increase comprehensibility.

The Affective Filter Hypothesis: Low Anxiety Is Conducive to Acquisition

The Affective Filter refers to the emotional state of the learner. To put it simply, when the L2 learner's anxiety, or filter level, is high, then it is difficult for her to acquire the new language. On the other hand, when the learner is motivated and confident—the filter level is low—she acquires the new language more easily. An encouraging and relaxing atmosphere may lower the learner's affective filter, creating conditions conducive to language learning. Recognizing the L2 writer's strengths and complimenting him on them is one way a tutor can make the student feel confident in his writing ability.

It is worth noting that Krashen does not deny the value of grammar teaching in language pedagogy for high school and college students, but he does not assume that the rules students *learned* will become *acquired.*[9] As an L2 learner, I have studied grammar in a non-English-speaking environment as well as lived in an English-speaking environment for quite a few years; my competence probably comes from both explicit learning and implicit acquisition. Though Krashen believes learning does not turn into acquisition, I believe my explicit grammar knowledge gained earlier has facilitated my second language acquisition later in my life. I don't always have to rely on others' paraphrasing to make input comprehensible. Sometimes I have been able to understand the input by analyzing its structure. For instance, once when I heard a phrase, "to zero in on," my first reaction was that I had hardly ever used two prepositions (*in* and *on*) together. Next, I figured that "to zero in on" must be an idiomatic expression, and the *on* indicates the direction. After I analyzed the structure and figured out the meaning from the context, the use of two prepositions started making sense to me, and I was able to pick up the use of this idiomatic expression without much trouble. In my case, learning, if not being able to turn into acquisition, at least facilitates acquisition.

So far, we have examined two views of how people learn a second language—habit formation and innatist. We will now turn to psychological and interactionist views. As you have probably observed already, each of these views forms one piece of the puzzle.

Cognitivist—Noticing Is Important

Second language acquisition scholars have also been influenced by cognitive psychology in explaining how people learn a second language. From this perspective, language learning is similar to learning other skills and involves these steps:

noticing → practicing → making the skill automatic

Noticing is an indispensable first step.[10] Learning an odd spelling of a word usually begins with noticing it when it appears in print, for example. To help the learner notice a word or phrase, a tutor may highlight it by pointing to it, saying it with a raising intonation, or underlining it. The learner may attempt to correct his own error when she notices the tutor's highlighting. If not, the tutor may give more help, such as grammatical commentary, to enhance noticing.

When learning a second language, learners move from *controlled processing* (paying attention) to *repeated activation* (practicing) to *automatization* (being available very rapidly whenever called on). To attain fluency, the learner needs to make many component, or supporting, skills automatic.[11] Like a driver who does not need to consciously recall all the component skills, such as when to turn the wheel or when to use the accelerator, a language learner can be fluent only when she does not need to think about component skills such as agreement and word order before she speaks.

During the learning process, the learner's new language system may be restructured due to the increased knowledge. When this occurs, the learner may make impressive progress at some times and backslide at other times. For example, a student who has used the word *came* correctly for several months may backslide to say *comed* after learning how to use the past tense *-ed* form before finally returning to the correct use of *came* with a new understanding. When this happens, it is actually a sign of the learner's language development. It may be the reason why a student begins making mistakes that he does not usually make.

When a controlled sequence becomes automatized, it is difficult to modify. This helps to explain the concept of fossilization, or persistent error. Based on McLaughlin's model, fossilization occurs when the learner's language becomes automatized before it is nativelike.[12] To prevent fossilization, some researchers say that error correction and grammar instruction are necessary,[13] but other researchers question the value of error correction since findings on its effectiveness have been inconsistent.[14]

Tutors may wonder if error correction really works because L2 writers often seem to repeat the same error even after correction. As an L2 learner, I feel it is important to remember that the process of moving from noticing to reactivation to automatization takes time. The cognitive process is often hidden, and the effect is not immediate. For instance, I used to write "to emphasize on . . . " without any awareness that it was wrong until a professor crossed out the *on* in my writing. This explicit error correction enhanced my *noticing* of the correct usage. A few days later, I noticed that I had written "to emphasize on . . . " in a paper. Later, as I was writing an e-mail, I noticed that I was typing "emphasize on" once more and I deleted the *on* immediately. Though I had been corrected once, I repeated the same error twice. However, I was aware of the error after I made it the second time. My self-correction happened sooner after each time. Based on the recent psychological views of language learning, I would say that I started restructuring my interlanguage (developing language), but my production of the correct form had not yet become automatized. Through repeated activation, that is, repeatedly using the word and self-correcting the error, the correct form gradually became stabilized. Now, every time I use the word *emphasize*, I feel as if there is a spotlight shining on it, and I always use it correctly.

Looking back, I am sure I had seen or heard the word *emphasize* used correctly countless times in context, but I did not pick up the correct form. Why? The answer may be that one of its synonyms, *focus*, is followed by *on*. It was not until my professor's correction that I realized that there was a gap between my usage and the target form. It took me quite a while to produce the correct form automatically. If you have ever watched a duck swimming, you will notice that the duck does not move fast. Sometimes it looks as though it is not moving at all. What you cannot see, however, is the duck's webbed feet paddling under the surface of the water. Likewise, what is happening in the L2 learner's mind is like the duck's webbed feet paddling in the water. It is not noticeable, but with time and practice, the learner does make progress and errors are less likely to become fossilized.

Interactionist—It Helps to Talk with an Expert

Interactionist theorists state that acquiring a second language takes place mainly through interaction. These theorists think that understanding is necessary in L2 acquisition, but their concern is how to make input understandable.[15] While using easier vocabulary and grammatical forms in place of more sophisticated ones can improve comprehensibility, learners may miss out on opportunities to learn more advanced forms. But with interactional or conversational modification between learners and more proficient speakers—like tutors—the more advanced forms become easier to understand, and the learners' attention is drawn to them.[16]

Interestingly, when the L2 learner notices that the new language does not make sense to her, or when her writing confuses a tutor, she might come to the realization that she needs to make some changes in the way she understands or uses the new language.[17] Tutors can facilitate this by using interactional tactics such as checking comprehension, requesting clarification, confirming meaning, self-repeating, and paraphrasing.[18] Here is an example of interactional modification between Hui, an ESL writer, and Dan, a tutor:

Hui: For me to pass the college entrance exam, I had to study hardly.

Dan: [clarification] You mean the college entrance exam was very easy?

Hui: [clarification] No, no. I read my book *hardly*. I studied ten hours every day.

Dan: [elaboration, clarification/confirmation] Are you saying you *studied a lot* in order to pass the college entrance exam?

Hui: [modification] Yes, I studied very much.

Dan: [confirmation] Oh, OK, I see what you mean.
[clarification] You had to *study hard* in order to pass the college entrance exam. You see, *hardly* means "almost never."

Hui: [modification] Then, I studied *hard* to pass the exam.

Essentially, interactional modifications give learners opportunities to pay attention to potentially troublesome parts of their L2 production. Through clarification and modification of the message, L2 learners have a chance not only to hear the words or grammatical structures they wish to know, but also to notice the features in their developing L2 that need to be corrected or modified.

Another perspective on the role of interaction in SLA is Lev Vygotsky's social cultural theory of cognitive development.[19] Vygotsky's work may be familiar to tutors who are education majors. While Vygotsky's theory usually refers to the ways children learn, it has been applied to adults' SLA.[20] In this view, second language learning takes place while the learner interacts with an expert (a tutor or teacher). Such interaction is helpful when it is appropriate to the learner's current and potential level of development, or what Vygotsky called the learner's *zone of proximal development* (ZPD).[21] To determine a student's ZPD, the tutor can talk with the student and find out precisely what he is able to do without help and what he can accomplish with assistance. The example below shows how a tutor, Michelle, applies the concept of ZPD in assisting an ESL student, Reiko:

Michelle: Tell me what you found out. [finding out what the learner can say without help]

Reiko: I found out that the earth is getting hot every year.

Michelle: The earth is getting . . . ? [finding out if the learner can do self-correction]

Reiko: The earth is getting warmer every year. [successful self-correction]

Michelle: And scientists call that . . . ? [finding out what the learner can say without help]

Reiko: Green room effect.

Michelle: Green room effect? [finding out if the learner can do self-correction]

Reiko: Yes. [confirmation]

Michelle: You mean the green house effect. [providing help when the learner was not able to do self-correction]

Reiko: Yes, yes, the green house effect. [reformulation]

In the example, Michelle figured out what Reiko was able to do with and without assistance. Michelle provided help, a word choice correction, for Reiko because word choice problems are often difficult for L2 writers to self-correct. As a result, Reiko improved her English when she talked with Michelle. This is also a good example of how the talk that occurs in tutoring sessions can be just as important as the writing.

This chapter has provided a summary of four of the major views on how L2 learners process second languages in their minds as they learn. From this chapter, it is clear that understanding how ESL learners learn English is not a simple matter.

L2 learners' unconventional word order and word choice may be attributed to their L1 influence or lack of experience in hearing and using English in their daily lives. Prepositions, articles, and idiomatic expressions are particularly difficult areas for learners whose L1 is very different from English.

Some L2 learners' errors seem resistant to correction. It is possible that (1) the wrong usages have become fossilized or (2) if not, the cognitive change (in restructuring the interlanguage) is taking place but is unobservable, or the effect has not yet appeared. In addition, L2 learners' intuition for what sounds right or wrong is often different from that of the native speaker's. Therefore, when they do not know the grammar rules or their hypotheses of how English works are false, they will not be able to detect their errors no matter how many times they read their writing aloud, which is also a reason why their errors persist. Furthermore, backsliding, insufficient monitoring, and stress also bear on the persistence of errors. Tutors should remember that second language learning never proceeds in a linear, smooth manner. Learners may backslide and use a wrong form due to their overuse of a new grammar rule. They may also forget to follow certain grammatical rules when they are not fully monitoring or when they are under stress.

To make English learning easier for L2 writers, tutors have many options, including

- recognizing learners' strengths
- providing a friendly and encouraging ambiance in the writing center
- drawing learners' attention to the target structure they need to learn
- having conversations with learners to figure out what they can do with or without assistance
- providing appropriate help at the right time

SLA research is fast growing and fascinating. In this chapter, I have shared with you some major theories of SLA and illustrated them with some of my personal experiences and those of other L2 learners. Interested readers may find more information about SLA in publications by, for example, Rod Ellis, Rosamond Mitchell and Florence Myles, and Patsy Lightbown and Nina Spada.

Notes

1. Rod Ellis (1994) indicates that a thorough approach to second language acquisition (SLA) covers (1) the black box (learner language processing mechanisms in the mind), (2) individual learner factors (e.g., age, sex, motivation), and (3) environmental factors (e.g., social settings). All three aspects interact. Some aspects are more controversial than others. For example, not all researchers agree that individual learner factors have a direct impact on language processing. Due to space limits, this chapter will discuss only some major theories of the first of these approaches, the black box. To explain learner language processing mechanisms, I follow Patsy Lightbown and Nina Spada's categorization of views. See Lightbown and Spada (1999, 35–45).

2. The Contrastive Analysis Hypothesis (CAH) is usually attributed to Robert Lado's work in 1957. See Lado, 2.

3. Chomsky, 32.

4. Buell.

5. Corder, 167.

6. Krashen, 26–27.

7. Mar. 17, 2002, personal communication with Krashen.

8. Reid, 3–17.

9. Mar. 17, 2002, personal communication with Krashen.

10. Schmidt, 129–158.

11. Mclaughlin, 133–34.

12. Mitchell and Myles, 86.

13. Higgs and Clifford, 57–80.

14. Truscott (1996).

15. Long and Robinson (1998).

16. Long and Robinson, 22.

17. Gass, Mackey, and Pica, 301.

18. Michael Long indicates that native speakers constantly modify their language when they talk with nonnative speakers. See Long (1983).

19. Vygotsky (1987), 21.

20. See, for example, Ohta, 54.

21. Vygotsky (1978), 84–91.

Works Cited

Buell, M. 2002. "I Know It's Wrong, but I Can't Show Why: Addressing Articles in Writing." In Panel: *Alternative Discourses, Alternative Languages: Taking Language Issues Seriously*. CCCC, Chicago, Illinois, March 22, 2002.

Chomsky, N. 1965. *Aspects of the Theory of Syntax*. Cambridge, MA: MIT Press.

Corder, S. P. 1967. "The Significance of Learners' Errors." *International Review of Applied Linguistics* 4: 161–70.

Ellis, R. 1994. *The Study of Second Language Acquisition*. Oxford: Oxford University Press.

Gass, S. M., A. Mackey, and T. Pica. 1998. "The Role of Input and Interaction in Second Language Acquisition." *The Modern Language Journal* 82 (3): 299–305.

Higgs, T., and R. Clifford. 1982. "The Push Toward Communication." In *Curriculum, Competence, and the Foreign Language Teacher*, edited by Theodore V. Higgs, 57–80. Skokie, IL: National Textbook Company.

Krashen, S. 1983. *The Natural Approach*. Hayward, CA: Alemany Press.

Lado, Robert. 1957. *Linguistics Across Cultures: Applied Linguistics for Language Teachers*. Ann Arbor, MI: University of Michigan.

Lightbown, P., and N. Spada. 1999. *How Languages Are Learned*. Oxford: Oxford University Press.

Long, M. H. 1983. "Native Speaker/Non-Native Speaker Conversation and the Negotiation of Comprehensible Input." *Applied Linguistics* 4: 126–41.

Long, M. H., and P. Robinson. 1998. "Focus on Form: Theory, Research, and Practice." In *Focus on Form in Classroom Second Language Acquisition*, edited by C. Doughty and J. Williams, 15–41. Cambridge: Cambridge University Press.

McLaughlin, B. 1987. *Theories of Second Language Learning*. London: Edward Arnold.

Mitchell, R., and F. Myles. 1998. *Second Language Learning Theories*. New York: Oxford University Press.

Ohta, A. S. 2000. "Rethinking Interaction in SLA: Developmentally Appropriate Assistance in the Zone of Proximal Development and the Acquisition of L2 Grammar." In *Sociocultural Theory and Second Language Learning*, edited by James P. Lantolf, 51–78. Oxford: Oxford University Press.

Reid, J. 1998. "'Eye' Learners and 'Ear' Learners: Identifying the Language Needs of International Students and U.S. Resident Writers." In *Grammar in the Composition Classroom*, edited by J. Reid and P. Byrd, 3–17. Boston: Heinle and Heinle.

Schmidt, R. 1990. "The Role of Consciousness in Second Language Learning." *Applied Linguistics* 11: 129–58.

Truscott, J. 1996. "The Case Against Grammar Correction in L2 Writing Classes." *Language Learning 46* (2): 327–69.

Vygotsky, L. S. 1978. *Mind in Society*. Cambridge, MA: Harvard University Press.

———. 1987. *The Collected Works of L. S. Vygotsky. Volume 1. Thinking and Speaking*. New York: Plenum Press.

3

Getting Started

Shanti Bruce

When most students enter one-to-one tutoring situations for the first time, they expect tutors to manage introductions and dictate the way their sessions will go. While tutees often behave like guests and need to be introduced to the writing center and the conferencing process on their first visit, on subsequent visits they may continue to take their cues from tutors. Even when students become familiar with the conferencing process, they may continue to be shy about starting or wait for the tutor to begin out of respect. For all of these reasons, tutors who know how to take the first step, to bring the writer into the conference by offering a friendly greeting and finding a comfortable place to meet, will put students at ease by showing them that they are a welcome part of this peer tutoring duo. This is true for U.S. students and even more so for international ones.

Getting started is often the hardest part of any task or assignment, and it is especially so for English as a second language (ESL) students. The reasons for this are varied, but for many students they include feeling intimidated, fearing being judged, worrying about taking risks, or being unfamiliar with the assignment. These reasons account for many of the students who put off going to the writing center. Aside from procrastination, some students are just not convinced that a visit to the writing center will be worthwhile. They may also feel that a tutoring conference will be uncomfortable and even scary. They may be afraid to take that first step of walking into the writing center—an unfamiliar place where it is hard to blend into the background and remain anonymous. Just by walking in the door, students are admitting to themselves and everyone there that they need help.

Sami, an ESL student from Saudi Arabia, is a prime example of this conundrum: he needs the help the writing center offers, but he is uncomfortable admitting it. (I discuss my meeting with Sami in Chapter 15.) He revealed that asking for help is actually a cultural taboo for many Arab male students. He explained how the writing center made him uneasy because it was a public place where other students could see that he needed help. For Sami, working with someone privately was the only answer because he feared the shame of being perceived as weak by others. In Chapter 1, Nancy Hayward explores the fear of appearing weak, and in her section on intercultural communication, she discusses beliefs about accepting or demanding help.

In general, international students have had little experience with writing centers. For them, the concept of shared responsibility for writing is often alien. In Chapter 13, Gerd Bräuer says that most ESL students have no idea what a writing center is or how it functions, and because of that, many of them end up avoiding writing centers all together.

Aware of the uncertainty many ESL students feel about coming to the writing center, tutors have a special obligation to help reduce this anxiety. But how do they do this? One way is to take a few minutes at the beginning of each session to make a plan: to set goals for the conference and discuss ways to accomplish those goals. It is important to note that planning, prioritizing, goal setting, and sticking to a schedule are all markedly Western in nature. The writing center has in many ways become a microcosm of U.S. society, an artifact of the culture, where values such as education for everyone, punctuality, taking turns, and staying on schedule are enacted everyday.

Making a plan is not just helpful for the student, but it can make the tutor's job easier as well. It creates a shared responsibility for how the session will unfold, and it reduces uncertainty about what to do next. When the tutor and student make the plan together, the responsibility for the session is shared, and the tutor doesn't have to worry that she is entirely liable for its outcome. "The student's contributions in these opening minutes," Thomas Newkirk explains, "need to be used to give the conference a mutually agreeable and mutually understood direction."[1] By collaboratively setting goals and creating a visual representation of them on a map at the beginning of a session, the expectations for the conference will be clear and shared.

Tika, an ESL student from Indonesia, shared her first writing center experience with me. In her account, she expresses many of the common fears students have about entering a writing conference, and her statement reminds us of how important it is to make an effort to put students at ease when they visit the writing center.

I was ready to go there, but I hesitated because there was an afraid feeling inside me. I was so nervous, tense, uneasy—it was a mixed feeling. But then, I would like to experience this new thing because universities in Indonesia don't have this service.

When I was approaching the door, I could hear my heart beating so fast. I didn't know what to expect, and there were so many questions in my mind: "What should I tell them when they ask me about my writing? Can I understand when they speak?" I found that most Americans speak very fast like a

Concorde jet! That makes me more nervous. "Are they patient people? Would they understand when I speak?" I tend to beat around the bush rather than get to the point. That is definitely a cultural matter! "What if they find that my writing was really bad, would they laugh at it or get angry at me?" In my country, it's embarrassing to make mistakes.

Having lots of questions made me uneasy.

When the tutor called my name, I was just like, "This is it. Whatever will be will be!" I was trying to comfort myself.

The tutor greeted me and complimented my jacket. We had a very short conversation. Was it an ice-breaker? After that, I found myself totally involved with the conference—no worries anymore.

Tika candidly recounted her feelings as she approached her first tutoring session. While some students want to avoid the writing center, many native English speakers (NES) and ESL students are similar to Tika in that they look forward to getting help at the writing center but are unsure of how things will go. Days of stress and apprehension were eased as the tutor casually greeted Tika and began a conversation by offering a positive comment, in this case a compliment on an article of clothing. Showing interest in the student can ease a tense situation and make her feel welcome.

Once introductions have been made and pleasantries exchanged, it is time to focus on the work of the tutoring session. To do that, you need to make a plan. Many tutors skip this step thinking they can just plunge right in because tutoring sessions have become so routine for them, because they think they know what is best, or because they think it will save time to skip that first step. Tutors may also fear the rigidity of outlining the way the session will go. But this is a mistake. Making a plan will give the conference direction while allowing the tutor to bond with the tutee right from the beginning by deciding and sharing a common goal. Also, organization does not preclude flexibility, and it actually saves time.

Make a Plan

Why Is This Important?

If you don't take the time to get organized and set goals, you might not use your time together effectively. "It might seem a little odd to make a plan for how you will spend the next 30 minutes together," says William J. Macauley, Jr., "But there is a worse problem: looking back at the past half hour and realizing you went practically nowhere with your tutoring session because you never really thought about where you wanted to end up."[2]

Since not all cultures prefer the westernized manner of getting right down to business, an explanation of the time allotted for the session may help the student see the need for an organized plan. Students usually come to the writing center with specific requests in mind, and it is best to give them a chance to discuss what they perceive are their most pressing needs at the beginning. That way, you will both be sure to consider them when planning the session.

NES and ESL students regularly come to the writing center wanting tutors to check their papers for grammar errors. While many of these students are unfamiliar with writing terminology and simply do not know how to ask for help with anything else, we can't always dismiss this request in favor of what we may consider the higher order concerns to be. For many ESL students, grammar may in fact be a higher order concern. For example, almost all Asian students have problems with personal pronouns and articles, and Chinese students have difficulty with verb tenses and verb endings because these are not features of their native languages. Offering suggestions for alternatives to focusing on grammar is beneficial, but we also need to trust our students and be willing to explore grammar concerns with them.

When asking for help with grammar, NES and ESL students tend to mean different things. NES typically want assistance with editing and correctness, whereas ESL students, who are often very knowledgeable about the language and its grammar rules, generally want to make sure they are saying things the way a NES would. Many ESL students have difficulty with collocations and receive comments from professors indicating that their phrasing "just isn't right." When these variations confuse their intended meanings, these seemingly lower order concerns actually rise to utmost importance. However, along with Ben Rafoth in Chapter 9, I caution tutors not to attempt to fix every phrase just because it sounds different. Sometimes, these variations can be refreshing, if not poignant, and leaving them intact goes a long way toward preserving the student's voice. For example, in Chapter 6, Amy Jo Minett shares one of her ESL student's "lovely if confusing" sentences. Her student wrote, "I do not want to know the earth ache."[3] The phrasing is at once unusual and moving.

If you do decide together that looking at grammar is the goal, or one of the goals of the session, keep in mind that even checking grammar requires a plan. If you skip this step and plunge right in thinking you can just tackle errors as they come, you will quickly get bogged down. Some of the paper may get edited, but it is unlikely that students will leave with any new understanding of grammar rules or editing techniques that they can do on their own. Taking the time to read a bit of the paper and decide which errors are most important and persistent is a more organized and productive approach. Cynthia Linville offers strategies for helping ESL students become proficient self-editors in Chapter 8. But remember, editing an entire paper in one session is not feasible and would ultimately produce a better piece of writing instead of a better writer. Some ESL students can become consumed by wanting to get their papers *fixed* and lose sight of the big picture; in other words, a tutoring session isn't just about one particular paper; it's about learning expectations for writing in English and learning how to prioritize issues (global before local). A tutor helps ESL students understand how to navigate the English language and the cultural and educational expectations that go along with it. It may be necessary to explain that setting goals for the session will benefit their writing in the long run. But believing that a plan is good is one thing, making the plan is another.

How Do I Do This?

To make an effective plan, first ask the writer a few questions about her work and her expectations for the session. Using the writer's responses, set the goals for the session collaboratively, sketch a map that will illustrate those goals, and finally, be ready to change the plan as the need arises.

One of the first questions to ask is whether the student is familiar with the writing center. If not, take the time to explain the peer tutor format, the goal-setting process, and any other techniques that could be used, such as reading the draft aloud (see Chapter 4) or serving as a scribe while clarifying meanings (see Chapter 7). Explaining how the writing center and the tutoring conference typically operate can go a long way toward easing a student's anxiety. In Chapter 13, Gerd Bräuer discusses the rarity of writing centers abroad and how new the concept is for most ESL writers.

These initial questions should be followed by more specific questions about the student's piece of writing. Regarded as one of the masters of the tutoring conference, Donald Murray suggests asking "questions which draw helpful comments out of the student writer" such as:

- "What did you learn from this piece of writing?"
- "What do you intend to do in the next draft?"
- "What do you like best in the piece of writing?"
- "What questions do you have of me?"[4]

ESL students may never have been asked questions like these about a piece of writing, so be patient if the answers don't come easily. Asking open-ended questions will help you to learn more about the writer as well as the assignment and the draft so far. Maintaining a dialogue will also reinforce the writer's responsibility in the conference.

If you have not gotten enough specific information, you may need to ask more direct questions. Paula Gillespie and Neal Lerner offer three basic questions that will get right to the point:

- "What was the assignment?"
- "What is your central point or main argument?"
- "What concerns you, or what do you want me to pay careful attention to?"[5]

The first question will familiarize you with the student's task, and the second will give you insight into how the student has approached the task. The second question skillfully avoids using the term *thesis*, which could be troubling for some students. The last question brings us to the next step in the process: setting the goals for the session. Let the writer know that his input is important. Remember, the best kind of plan is the one that tutor and tutee devise together. However, tutors should be prepared for ESL students who are uncomfortable or unwilling to take an active role because they see the tutor as the authority. These students may insist on repeatedly asking a tutor what she thinks and might leave the tutoring session feeling it was a waste of time if the tutor refuses to do or say anything directive. In these cases, the tutor can take the lead, and with multiple visits, these students will likely become accustomed to actively participating in writing center tutorials.

If the student only wants an editing session and you feel that she would benefit from spending time on more global concerns, you could acknowledge the student's request and add a request of your own. Your ideas are valuable to the student and to the success of the session. You could say, "OK, we will address one or two grammar issues, but if I see any unclear meanings, we will take a look at them as well." Collaboration fosters a dialogue that will help to develop trust between tutor and tutee, while preserving the student's ownership of the piece and responsibility in the session. "When the map is negotiated," says Macauley, the session is planned "without either dominating the session."[6]

The number of goals for each session will vary. There is no set formula for determining how many items you will have time to address. With practice, you will become more accurate at gauging the amount of time certain goals take. If global writing concerns are on the agenda, tackling one or two goals will probably be all you can expect to cover. If issues of mechanics are to be the focus, you may have time to cover two, three, or even four goals. Sometimes it is okay to overplan because it will remind the student of items that still need attention after the conference ends.

Once you have both become stakeholders in the conference by agreeing on a set of goals, it is time to make the plan visible. Methods such as listing, clustering, and formal and informal outlining are familiar to ESL students, but there are also ways to be creative in visually representing the goals for the session. Creative representations aid visual learners, and for ESL students, where language fails, visuals can fill in. A sociolinguistics professor shared an anecdote with me about a graduate ESL student who was having trouble grasping the concept of an overarching idea. She said she finally turned the student's paper over and drew a picture of an umbrella. She wrote the broad idea across the umbrella and then filled in all of the different components that made up the idea underneath. She said the student caught on immediately.

Visual representations of plans for tutoring sessions can take many forms. Play with different ideas and see which ones work for you and the students you meet. If a situation calls for a hierarchical representation of goals, you could try drawing a triangle where the top point represents your top priority for the conference, and the bottom two corners represent secondary concerns.

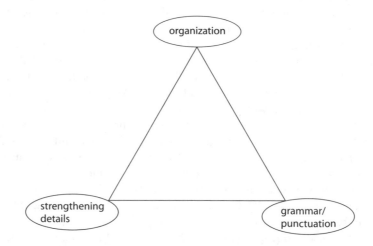

Or, if you decide to focus on goals of equal importance, a circle can be divided into halves, thirds, or fourths to represent equal goals.

It may not be possible to fill in the specific grammar, punctuation, or formatting goals for the session until you read some of the student's paper. The student may be unaware of these issues and therefore unable to tell you about them at the beginning of the session.

Once you have an idea of what type of visual aid will work best for the goals you have established, sketch an outline of it on a piece of paper so that it remains visible throughout the conference. Explain the sketch to the student and how it represents the goals for the conference. Involve him in the process by inviting him to help fill in the sketch with the goals.

Points to Remember

Let the plan guide you, but remember to remain flexible. While making a plan is important, writing and conferencing are, without a doubt, unpredictable processes. "A tutoring session," Donald A. McAndrew and Thomas J. Reigstad explain, "shows emergent adaptation as the session is negotiated and defined through the conversation of tutor and writer."[7] Refer to your map, but don't be afraid to revise it: add to it, scratch out items, arrow in new items, circle or highlight items that emerge as the most important, and star items that you probably won't get to cover so that the student will remember to address these issues on her own.

It will be easy to assess what you have accomplished during the conference by referring back to the map as the session concludes. You can go over it together and check off the items you have completed, or if you checked them off along the way, you can enjoy reviewing how much you covered during the session. Even if you only got to a couple of items, it will be pleasing to know that one or two of the goals you set were covered completely. Again, it is important to note that the pleasure of checking off items on the to-do list is Western in nature. "We are a doing society rather than a being society," Nancy Hayward asserts, "We are judged and we judge people on their accomplishments."[8]

If you haven't done so already, explain to the student that the value of the map extends far beyond this single tutoring session. It will serve as a guide when he revises the paper on his own, and it could give him ideas for outlining and goal setting for his next assignment. It will help tutors as well when it comes to filling out faculty reports or writing center logs on student conferences. Going over the map at the end of the session will provide a visual representation of what has been accomplished and will bring closure to the conference while providing the student with direction for the revisions she will now make on her own.

Most important, remember that when you tutor ESL students you are dealing with much more than main ideas and verb endings. You are helping to further introduce a student to U.S. cultural and educational expectations.

Notes

1. Newkirk, 313.

2. Macauley, 1.

3. Minett, Chapter 6, 61.

4. Murray, 68.

5. Gillespie and Lerner, 26.

6. Macauley, 3.

7. McAndrew and Reigstad, 28.

8. Hayward, personal communication, Dec. 11, 2003.

Works Cited

Gillespie, Paula, and Neal Lerner. 2000. *The Allyn and Bacon Guide to Peer Tutoring.* Boston: Allyn and Bacon.

Macauley, William J., Jr. 2000. "Setting the Agenda for the Next 30 Minutes." In *A Tutor's Guide: Helping Writers One to One,* edited by Ben Rafoth, 1–8. Portsmouth, NH: Boynton/Cook.

McAndrew, Donald A., and Thomas J. Reigstad. 2001. *Tutoring Writing: A Practical Guide for Conferences.* Portsmouth, NH: Boynton/Cook.

Murray, Donald M. 2000. "The Listening Eye: Reflections on the Writing Conference." In *The Writing Teacher's Sourcebook*. 4th ed. Edited by Edward P. J. Corbett, Nancy Myers, and Gary Tate, 66–71. New York: Oxford University Press.

Newkirk, Thomas. 2001. "The First Five Minutes: Setting the Agenda." In *The Allyn and Bacon Guide to Writing Center Theory and Practice*, edited by Robert W. Barnett and Jacob S. Blumner, 302–15. Boston: Allyn and Bacon.

4

Reading an ESL Writer's Text*

Paul Kei Matsuda and Michelle Cox

In this chapter, we discuss the part of a writing center conference that is at the center of the conferencing process—the reading of the writer's draft. Although the process of reading may be the least visible part of the conference, it is one of the most important because it is during this process that tutors begin to formulate their initial responses to the text. In many cases, reading texts written by English as a second language (ESL) writers is not radically different from reading those written by native English-speaking (NES) writers; tutors can use many of the same principles and strategies they use in reading NES texts. Yet, because ESL writers often come from different linguistic, cultural, and educational backgrounds, some aspects of ESL writers' texts may stand out, especially to the eyes of native English speakers who do not have extensive background in working with ESL writers.

Some of the initial reactions to ESL writers' texts may be quite positive. Inexperienced readers of ESL texts may be fascinated by details about the ESL writer's native language, culture, or country, or stories of how they or their family came to the United States. Some may be intrigued by the extensive use of metaphors and figurative language in some ESL writers' texts. Others may be amazed by how much the writers have accomplished with a language they did not grow up with. Unfortunately, not all encounters with ESL texts produce such generous responses. Readers with little or no experience in working with ESL writers may be drawn to surface-level errors and differences that they see as problematic.

Readers may find differences between NES and ESL writers' texts at various levels—from word formation to sentence structure to organization. The texts may contain many errors, such as missing articles, "wrong" prepositions and verb endings, and unusual sentence structures that "just don't sound right."

* We thank Aya Matsuda and Kate Tirabassi for their critical and helpful comments and suggestion on an earlier version of this chapter.

The word choices may seem odd, or the use of idiomatic phrases may seem inappropriate. The organization of the text may not resemble what native English-speaking readers might expect. The thesis statement may be missing or located in places where the reader does not expect to find it, such as near the end of the paper. In a persuasive writing assignment, the writer's stance may not be clear. For a research paper assignment, the writer may have written a paper filled with allusive references without citing the sources.

Because of these and other differences, ESL writing is sometimes seen as "deficient," especially when it is evaluated in comparison with texts produced by NES writers. In "Toward an Understanding of the Distinct Nature of L2 Writing," Tony Silva synthesized research studies comparing ESL and NES writers and writing. The picture of ESL writers and their texts that emerged from the synthesis was overwhelmingly negative: Second language (L2) writing is "simpler and less effective (in the eyes of L1 [first language] readers) than L1 writing"; composing in an L2 is "more constrained, more difficult, and less effective"; "L2 writers' texts are less fluent (fewer words), less accurate (more errors), and less effective (lower holistic scores)."[1] As Silva points out, however, it may be unreasonable to use the same criteria to evaluate ESL texts and NES texts. Based on the findings of his review, Silva suggests the need to ask questions such as: "When does different become incorrect or inappropriate? and What is good enough?"[2]

It is important to realize that differences are not necessarily signs of deficiency. In fact, some of the differences may reflect the writer's advanced knowledge of conventions in other languages or in specific English discourse communities including disciplines with which the tutor may not be familiar. Yet, readers may find the differences distracting when, for example, the text contains certain kinds of errors or too many errors, or when the text is organized in ways that do not match a reader's understanding of the particular genre or other conventions. In some cases, the tutor may be drawn to those differences so strongly that they feel lost or frustrated; they may even feel unqualified to work with ESL writers. The initial fear that some tutors have in working with ESL writers is not insurmountable. Becoming familiar with some of the characteristics of ESL texts and their sources can help tutors work with ESL writers with more confidence, read beyond the differences, and recognize the strengths of those texts more easily.

Understanding ESL Writers' Texts

ESL writers and their texts vary widely from individual to individual and from situation to situation, and overgeneralization should be avoided. Still, it is useful to understand some of the general characteristics of many ESL writers' texts and various sources of influence. One of the important factors is the ESL writer's second-language proficiency. Many ESL writers are still in the process of developing the intuitive understanding of the English language—its structure and use—and for that reason, they may not be able to produce grammatical sentences as easily as NES writers can. As pointed out in the Conference on College Composition and Communication (CCCC) Statement on Second-Language Writing and Writers, "the acquisition of a second language and second-language literacy is a time-consuming process that will continue through students' academic careers and beyond. . . . Furthermore, most second-language writers are still in the process of acquiring syntactic and lexical competence—a process that will take a lifetime."[3] Because ESL writers often have not internalized some of the rules of grammar, they are often not able to identify errors on their own by, for example, reading the text aloud.

Although language proficiency affects the overall quality of ESL texts, the relationship between language proficiency and writing proficiency is not simple; the ability to speak English does not necessarily correspond directly with the quality of texts they produce.[4] Even ESL writers who do not seem to be able to communicate their thoughts in spoken English may be able to write prose that puts many NES writers to shame. This is the case with some international students who have learned English mostly through the medium of writing. Other students are more fluent in spoken English—they may be familiar with a wide variety of colloquial and idiomatic expressions—but they may still produce texts that do not seem to reflect the high level of their spoken fluency. This is typical of so-called "Generation 1.5 writers"—ESL students who have lived in an English-dominant society for a number of years and acquired English primarily through spoken interactions. Needless to say, these are extreme cases; most ESL writers fall somewhere in between.

ESL writers' texts are also shaped in part by their prior experiences with literacy. While some ESL writers may have received extensive instruction in writing, others have been schooled in educational systems that did not focus on composition. Some ESL writers are highly experienced—even published—writers in other languages; others have not received instruction in writing beyond the sentence level. Some ESL writers may even be native speakers of a language that does not have a written form. Research on contrastive rhetoric suggests that writers' linguistic, cultural, and educational backgrounds may influence texts in various ways as "the nature and functions of discourse, audience, and persuasive appeals often differ across linguistic, cultural and educational contexts."[5]

It is important to remember that these generalizations do not apply to all ESL students, and that not all differences can be attributed to differences in ESL writers' native language or cultural background. The lack of organization in some ESL texts, as Bernard Mohan and Winnie Au-Yeung Lo have pointed out, may be a result of the overemphasis on grammar in some educational systems.[6] International students, who learn English as a foreign language while in their native country, may have been taught how to compose English sentences but not necessarily entire compositions. As Carol Severino points out in "The 'Doodles' in Context," "organization is often the last feature to be taught and learned in both first- and second-language writing, if it is taught at all."[7] Experience with composing grammatical sentences, however, does not lead directly to the ability to compose full compositions.

Ways of Reading Difference

In "The Sociopolitical Implications of Response to Second Language and Second Dialect Writing," Carol Severino draws on Min-Zhan Lu's framework in describing three stances that readers can take when responding to ESL texts: assimilationist, accommodationist, and separatist. When a reader takes an assimilationist stance, the reader's goal is to help the ESL writer "write linear, thesis-statement and topic-sentence-driven, error-free, and idiomatic English as soon as possible,"[8] encouraging the writer and their text to assimilate into the dominant culture. The assimilationist, then, reads differences as deficiencies—errors to be corrected.

Readers who take an accommodationist stance may also try to teach the NES norm, but their goal is different from that of the assimilationist. The accommodationist reader's goal is to help the writer learn new discourse patterns without completely losing the old, so that the writer can maintain both their L1 and L2 linguistic and cultural identities. The accommodationist, then, reads differences as, well, differences, explaining to the writer how some differences may be seen as deficiencies by some readers; it is up to the writer "how much like a native speaker" he wants to sound.[9]

When readers take a separatist stance, their goal is farther away from the assimilationist goal of teaching ESL writers to write like NES writers. The separatist reader's goal is to support the writer in maintaining separate linguistic and cultural identities, and to advocate for NES readers to read ESL texts "generously" with more appreciation for multicultural writing. The separatist, then, reads to overlook, and therefore preserve, difference.

The stances come down to ways of reading difference, and whether tutors should read to "correct" difference, explain difference, or overlook difference. Severino provides three scenarios, showing how she, when conferencing in the writing center, shifted between stances in relation to the writers' goals and situations. When working with Takaro, a Generation 1.5 student, Severino took an accommodationist approach, focusing first on what Takaro was communicating through the writing, explaining how rhetorical choices are related to situation and audience. When working with Michael, a speaker of a nondominant variety of English, Severino took a separatist approach during the first few sessions—focusing on what Michael was communicating and encouraging confidence in writing—and then moved toward an accommodationist approach later, to help Michael see how various audiences would read his writing.

In each case, Severino steered clear of the assimilationist stance. She had felt tempted to take this stance after first reading Michael's writing, as she felt "stunned" by the number of errors in the text. However, she resisted the urge in order to remain consistent with the writing center pedagogy. Instead, she "responded to his piece as an act of communication, which it was, rather than as a demonstration of how well Michael knew and/or could apply the rules."[10]

Inexperienced readers of ESL texts tend to lean toward the assimilationist approach out of their desire to help ESL writers. In doing so, however, they inadvertently read difference as deficiency. As the reader makes the effort to move away from the deficiency model, however, they become more open to understanding their own responses to ESL writing and to learning from the writer. Today, many second-language writing specialists advocate for a broader definition of what counts as "good writing," urging NES readers to see "accented English" as part of that spectrum. In *Understanding ESL Writers*, Ilona Leki writes:

> ESL students can become very fluent writers of English, but they may never become indistinguishable from a native speaker, and it is unclear why they should. A current movement among ESL writing teachers is to argue that, beyond a certain level of proficiency in English writing, it is not the students' texts that need to change; rather it is the native-speaking readers and evaluators (particularly in educational institutions) that need to learn to read more broadly, with a more cosmopolitan and less parochial eye.[11]

According to Leki, the assimilationist goal of making ESL writing indistinguishable from NES writing is unrealistic. In many cases, the assimilationist stance is also undesirable because it leads to the imposition of the norms of dominant U.S. academic discourse as well as various cultural values that comes with it.

Resisting the Assimilationist Stance

Those who take the assimilationist stance do not always have malicious intent. As Severino suggests, people who take the assimilationist stance often do so in order to "smoothly blend or melt [the ESL writer and their text] into the desired discourse communities and avoid social stigma by controlling any features that[,] in the eyes of audiences with power and influence[,] might mark a writer as inadequately educated or lower class."[12] In other words, the assimilationist stance may be an attempt to protect the ESL writer from other readers—especially those readers who have institutional authority over ESL writers. Tutors may feel the same responsibility, and may try to represent what they consider to be the possible response from the intended audience of the ESL writer's text: the professor.

Sometimes ESL writers come into the writing center because they were told by their professors to visit the writing center to get their drafts "cleaned up" or to work on their "grammar." From these experiences with professors' reactions to ESL writing, tutors may believe that professors tend to be assimilationists. While there are professors who do approach ESL students with assimilationist intentions, several error gravity studies—studies that review which errors tend to attract more attention by specific groups of readers—show that many professors are more tolerant of differences in ESL writing, or at least of certain types of differences, than of those in NES writing.

Terry Santos, for example, showed that professors were able to overlook local errors—errors that do not directly affect meaning—such as articles, prepositions, spelling, comma splices, or pronoun agreement.[13] Studies of error gravity generally show that professors tend to react more negatively to global errors—errors that affect the comprehension of meaning—such as the wrong word choice, word order, and verb tenses.[14]

One of the implications of error gravity studies is that tutors may want to focus more of their attention on global errors rather than on local errors when reading ESL texts. It may not be possible to define global and local errors in terms of particular grammatical features because whether and how a particular error affects meaning depends on the context. Instead, tutors can prioritize their responses by paying attention to their own initial reactions to particular errors that seem to interfere with their understanding of the meaning of the text. As discussed in the next section, this approach applies not only to grammatical errors but also to other aspects of writing.

Reading Strategies

Though each writing center session demands different approaches, there is a general process of reading ESL writing that can be useful. It is generally a good idea to start with a quick reading of the ESL writer's text, focusing on what the writer is trying to communicate and how the paper is organized. A common practice among tutors is to ask writers to read their draft aloud during the conference, rather than the tutor read the draft silently. This strategy is often effective for NES writers who can use their intuitive sense of the grammar and the flow of English to assess their own writing. Many ESL writers, however, have not developed that intuitive sense of the English language. For many ESL writers, reading their paper out loud may shift their attention to the pronunciation of the English language—a proficiency separate from writing in English.

It may be more helpful for the ESL writer to hear the tutor read the paper out loud—to note when the reader stumbles, pauses, fills in missing articles and modifiers, or reads smoothly. The interpretation of meaning that takes place in the process of reading aloud "rhetorically with feeling and meaning" may also help the tutor identify where the writer's intended meaning is not clear to the tutor.[15] Yet, on the first reading, especially if the number of errors prevents the tutor from reading aloud without stumbling too often, it may be more effective for the tutor to read silently, which gives the reader time to sort through meaning.

Sometimes less experienced readers of ESL texts get so overwhelmed by the sheer number of errors that they have to give up on the draft and stop reading somewhere in the middle of the paper. However, if a paper isn't read to the end, the reader may miss out on information that could clarify the meaning or organization of the paper. The point of the paper may not become clear until the end if the text is organized inductively. Questions that arise in the tutor's mind while reading the beginning of the paper may be answered toward the end. Reading a piece of ESL writing in full allows the reader to come to an understanding of how the paper is organized on its own terms. Reading to the end of a piece of ESL writing is only beneficial if the reader can suspend judgment while reading—reading past variations in sentence structure, waiting to see how the writer will pull the paper together, maintaining an open mind when the writer's opinions and beliefs vary substantially from the tutor's.

Another feature of some ESL writing that may be disorienting is the lack of meta-discourse or signposts—the transitional words and sentences that move readers between ideas, and the structures that mark the organization of a text. Even though a text may not have an organization that is immediately recognizable, there may be an organization at work. The trick is to identify and piece together the logic that is not immediately apparent to the reader by formulating questions with the assumption that there is logic in it—by giving the writer the benefit of the doubt.

After reading the whole text for the gist, it is often a good idea to reread the text, this time placing brief marks—such as checkmarks or stars—near features or details that seem surprising or those that jar the reading process: the unexpected. It is the unexpected in ESL writing that can make reading ESL writing challenging, as it demands tutors become more aware of their tacit expectations for style, rhetorical choices, genre conventions, and relationships to audience. But it is also the unexpected that can teach tutors the most about their own responses to writing. Teachers often call the unexpected occurrences that happen in the classroom "teachable moments"—moments where significant learning could occur. It may be helpful to think of the unexpected in ESL writing with the same positive twist.

To capitalize on the unexpected, the tutor needs to be aware of his or her own responses as a reader. For instance, if a particular passage seems disorienting, the reader can take advantage of this situation by focusing on where he or she started feeling lost and why. What in the text caused the reader to wander? What is it about the reader's own expectations that contributed to the feeling of disorientation? The reader should also focus on areas where he or she feels "stuck"—unable to generate meaning from the text—and use this experience as an opportunity to consider what would be needed to move forward in the reading process. Does the reader need to ask the writer a question? Does the reader need to mark the area and then move on with reading, in the hope that another section of the paper will help the reader negotiate the challenging section?

Some of the unexpected features of ESL writing may be rich cultural details or unique perspectives that students bring with them. Making note of those details or perspectives that are particularly interesting or insightful to the tutor is useful in encouraging the ESL writer. Sometimes, however, readers of ESL texts can get distracted by their own curiosity about certain details, such as descriptions of unfamiliar places, cultures, and ways of thinking. While these details do make ESL writing compelling to read, they can also lead the tutor away from the writer's goals and more toward their own goals, which could include asking the writer about their cultures or experiences, leading the reader to become more a tourist than a tutor.

> People always pay attention to *how* I say things, and never listen to *what* I say.
> —an undergraduate ESL student

In this chapter we have suggested that, while ESL writers' texts may have features that are distinct from NES writers' texts due to many sources of influence, it is possible to read beyond the differences if the tutor can suspend judgments, focus on meaning, and be aware of their own preferences and biases. Ultimately, reading is an act of communication—the act of listening to what the writer has to say. When we listen—truly listen—we treat ESL writers with the respect they deserve, regarding them as peers rather than as uninformed learners of the English language and the U.S. culture. It is only in such an atmosphere of mutual respect that the collaborative pedagogy of the writing center can turn differences into opportunities for growth both for the reader and the writer.

Notes

1. Silva, 668.
2. Silva, 670.
3. CCCC Committee on Second Language Writing, 669–70.
4. Cumming, 81–141.
5. CCCC Committee, 670.
6. Mohan and Lo (1985).
7. Severino (1993a), 47.
8. Severino (1993b), 187.
9. Severino (1993b), 189.
10. Severino (1993b), 194.
11. Leki, 132–33.
12. Severino (1993b), 187.
13. Santos, 81.
14. Santos, 81; Vann, Meyer, and Lorenz, 432.
15. Severino (1993b), 190.

Works Cited

CCCC Committee on Second Language Writing. 2001. "CCCC Statement on Second-language Writing and Writers." *College Composition and Communication* 52 (4): 669–74.

Cumming, Alister. 1989. "Writing Expertise and Language Proficiency." *Language Learning* 39 (1): 81–141.

Leki, Ilona. 1992. *Understanding ESL Writers: A Guide for Teachers*. Portsmouth, NH: Heinemann.

Mohan, Bernard, and Winnie Au-Yeung Lo. 1985. "Academic Writing and Chinese Students: Transfer and Developmental Factors." *TESOL Quarterly* 19 (3): 515–34.

Santos, Terry. 1988. "Professors' Reactions to the Academic Writing of Nonnative-Speaking Students." *TESOL Quarterly* 22 (1): 69–90.

Severino, Carol. 1993a. "The 'Doodles' in Context: Qualifying Claims About Contrastive Rhetoric." *The Writing Center Journal* 14 (1): 44–62.

———. 1993b. "The Sociopolitical Implications of Response to Second Language and Second Dialect Writing." *Journal of Second Language Writing* 2 (3):187–201.

Silva, Tony. 1993. "Toward an Understanding of the Distinct Nature of L2 Writing: The ESL Research and Its Implications." *TESOL Quarterly* 27 (4): 657–77.

Vann, Roberta, Daisy Meyer, and Frederick Lorenz. 1984. "Error Gravity: A Study of Faculty Opinion of ESL Errors." *TESOL Quarterly* 18 (3): 427–40.

5

Avoiding Appropriation

Carol Severino

When I was studying Intermediate Italian in a study-abroad program in Italy, I wrote for our last assignment a brief essay "Un Viaggio a Venezia" about a trip to Venice I had taken some weeks before. In my simple syntax and vocabulary, I explained the theme of my mini travel essay: despite the fact that we travelers— four students, another professor, and I—had conflicting interests and itineraries, we managed to negotiate and compromise so each person could do or see one thing she wanted to. We managed to shop for jewelry, masks, and shoes, feed the pigeons on St. Mark's Square, eat pizza by the Grand Canal, and watch the parade of boats in celebration of the Feast of the Redeemer. I was proud of my composition because I felt I had successfully communicated a complex travel experience in a foreign language I had studied for less than a year.

The day after I returned to the United States, I received a friendly e-mail from my Italian teacher saying he had read and enjoyed my essay and had made just "a few corrections." When I opened the attachment and read my essay, I realized that not only had he taken the time to type directly in my hand-written essay, but he had, in fact, typed in a different essay—a more accurate and sophisticated one with vocabulary and verb tenses I did not know how to use yet. It was still more or less my experience in Venice, but now more in my teacher's language and my teacher's voice. For example, my original opening sentence had read, in translation:

> *Trips to foreign cities are always a challenge, but when there are many travelers, the challenges become greater.*

The revised sentence now read:

> *Trips in foreign lands are always challenging, but when the travelers are many, the challenges multiply.*

At the time I didn't know how to say either "challenging" or "multiply." I had also written, rather clumsily, *"Before the trip I had read my guidebook with a map,"* but in the new version, *"I had read my tourist guide and took a look at the topographical map."* Almost every sentence was changed and elevated to a higher register. I wondered if my original wordings were grammatically incorrect or just not as native- and mature-sounding as these new, improved ones. Perhaps my well-meaning, hard-working Italian teacher thought that it was inappropriate for a middle-aged American professor to sound like a grade-schooler. Realizing that his embarrassment for me might have motivated his editing, I felt ashamed of myself and the quantity and quality of his changes. Humbling second-language writing experiences such as this one (I have had many others) have enabled me to identify with the feelings of ESL writers who may also have overzealous teachers and tutors.

Reformulation and Appropriation

Helpful and generous as he was, my Italian teacher had revised my writing so it no longer sounded like me or reflected the state of my second language learning at the time. Ironically, I liked my original simple and nonidiomatic style; my hybrid Italian American voice expressed who I was and what I knew. On the other hand, I continue to learn from his edits; whenever I reread my transformed essay, I reinforce the authentic native expressions that real Italians use. The intent of my teacher's "few corrections," after all, was not to humble or discourage me, but to teach me the authentic Italian I needed to replace my interlanguage "Inglesiano."

Such language learning is the main justification for the teaching strategy that Andrew Cohen calls *reformulation* that my teacher used.[1] Recommended as an optional tutoring strategy for English a second language (ESL) students, reformulation means correcting and revising second language writing, making it not only more grammatical, but more idiomatic and native-sounding. Reformulating, in effect, involves "native-speaker-izing" second language writing—changing the wording so that the writing sounds more like first language writing. To be accurate in our discussion, though, we should posit a continuum of second and first language writing instead of thinking in terms of two different poles: L1 versus L2 writing. In this case, reformulation would be reducing a lesser to greater number of second language features by replacing them with a lesser to greater number of native language features. Thus, reformulation ranges from slight to extensive.

For example, here is a sentence that Satomi, an ESL writer working in our writing center, wrote in her personal essay about calligraphy for her Rhetoric class:

> *It is said that in Japan to write own names well is to represent how intelligent people are.*

Many options exist for revising Satomi's sentence—from correcting the only actual grammar error (*one's* own name versus *own names*) to reformulating and "naturalizing" the sentence with gerunds and eliminating the copula "is" and infinitive "to represent":

> *It is said in Japan that writing one's name well represents how intelligent people are.*

A second further reformulation would be to use the more idiomatic expression "a sign of" that might be in Satomi's passive but not active, working vocabulary:

> *It is said in Japan that writing one's name well is a sign of intelligence.*

Yet a third, more extreme option would be to eliminate the passive voice expression "It is said":

> *The Japanese say that writing one's name well is a sign of intelligence.*

Which reformulations would we say preserve Satomi's voice? Which distort or remove Satomi's voice? To what extent would such a judgment about the resulting voice depend on Satomi's input into the decisions of whether and how much to reformulate?

On some occasions, such as with my Italian essay, or perhaps with the third option for Satomi's sentence, when writing has been reformulated, we might evaluate the changed product as having been *appropriated*, or taken away from the student writer by the teacher, tutor, or editor. Appropriation usually involves the writer feeling, as I did when reading my Italian professor's corrections, a loss of voice, ownership, authorship, or emotional and intellectual connection to the writing and how it was composed. Such an event—when control of a text is removed from an author who then feels alienated from it—might be considered an "act of appropriation," although undoubtedly one can still learn language and about language use from the experience. On other occasions, however, when language has been reformulated in whole or in part by a teacher, tutor, or editor, for example, with the consent and participation of the student, we might conclude that the student's writing has not been appropriated. What are the situational factors that influence the evaluation of an act of reformation as appropriation or not? In this chapter, after giving a brief overview of the history of appropriation, I identify and discuss some of these situational factors with the help of tutors from the University of Iowa Writing Center, all of whom work intensively with ESL students.

Some Background on Appropriation

In Composition Studies, issues of appropriation first arose in relation to native speakers of English (L1 writers) and the topics and content of their papers. As Lil Brannon and Cy Knoblauch have pointed out, teachers often wrest the direction of their students' writing from them so that they will write about what interests the teachers instead of what interests the students. Then students are confused or demoralized by having to puzzle out their teachers' expectations and write to fulfill them instead of writing from their own impetus and intentions. Teachers appropriate or take over the texts of their students when they respond to their students' papers with their own Ideal Texts in mind instead of negotiating with the students about what the students' intentions are and how best to fulfill them.[2] Not only are students' texts removed from them by teachers, but more importantly, their control over these texts. Issues of appropriation, therefore, are usually issues of control over composing and revising. Who has more control of the text—the writer or the teacher or tutor? We can probably say that the more control the tutor, teacher, or editor has over the writer's text, the greater the likelihood of appropriation.

Control is also related to authority. Teachers take control of students' texts because they do not accord their students or their texts the authority they grant to canonical authors and their texts, according to Brannon and Knoblauch.[3] Rather than struggle to get meaning from opaque student texts as they would do with a William Faulkner or Dylan Thomas work, they assume control over those texts and over the writers themselves. Brannon and Knoblauch and others, such as Nancy Sommers[4] and Richard Straub,[5] have recommended that teachers relinquish some of their authority and control over the students' texts and return it to their students, thus empowering them. They recommend that teachers act as respondents, informing students of the effects of their intentions and words on them as readers. Most tutoring guides, such as those by Toni-Lee Capossela[6] and Paula Gillespie and Neal Lerner,[7] also recommend that tutors not interfere with their students' control of their texts. They advocate the tutor roles of collaborator, facilitator, coach, and consultant rather than more teacherly, controlling and directive roles of informant, editor, and evaluator.

Appropriation and Foreign and Second Language Writers

Well-meaning teachers and tutors can exert too much control over the topics, content, and development of their ESL students' papers, although the motivation for their assuming control may be different than it is with native speakers. The motivation to control may stem from disparity in cultural knowledge; either the tutor or student may have more cultural expertise, depending on the topic of the assignment. Sometimes the assignment situation seems to demand the tutor's directiveness. In our roles as cultural informants advocated by Judith Powers[8] and surrogate academic audience advocated by Joy Reid,[9] we tutors often know more about the assigned U.S. culture-bound topics of students' papers than our ESL students do, especially if they are international students who have lived for only a short time in the United States, but must still write convincingly about U.S. culture, history, or controversies. Unless students can interpret and stretch their assignments to compare, for example, birth control and reproduction in China with those practices in the United States, they may have no other choice but to use the tutor's background information or stance on these U.S. controversies. Sometimes it is only with the historical context and position provided by the tutor that the student is able to make sense of the material he has gathered from researching the controversy. This kind of assignment-induced appropriation often cannot be avoided without more widespread changes; writing programs would have to allow ESL students a choice of controversies and/or provide courses with international or multicultural curricula, such as those recommended by Paul Matsuda and Tony Silva.[10]

Ironically, a kind of reverse cultural appropriation can also occur when the topics for writing are from the student's own culture. In Composition and ESL classes and in writing centers such as ours in which ESL students do personal writing, well-meaning teachers and tutors often urge ESL students to write about (too) familiar topics such as the Moon Festival or Chinese New Year, even when, as Ilona Leki points out, those topics might be considered stale, providing little opportunity to discover new ideas and personal meaning.[11] Call it the equivalent of "What I Did on My Summer Vacation."

Most commonly, the issue of appropriating second language writing in general arises not in relation to control of topic or content, but to control of language. Here the disparity is in linguistic knowledge, not cultural knowledge; the linguistic repertoire of a tutor who is a native speaker of the language is far greater than that of her students. My Italian teacher was much more likely to exert control over my Italian phrasing than he was to ask or require me to write on a trip to Florence, or on an American holiday such as the Fourth of July. As a result of his elevating my style in the direction of his Ideal Text, some of my voice was sacrificed for increased vocabulary or, more precisely, passive vocabulary, because I cannot guarantee I will use those new expressions correctly when I try them in different contexts in the future.

The Trade-Off Between Voice and Authentic Language

I felt that some of the language of my travel essay had been appropriated and some of my voice was lost because I was satisfied with sounding like an American English speaker and Intermediate Italian learner in this foreign language situation; I had become accustomed to reading my personal writing in L1 or L2 in a possibly self-indulgent manner—as if I were looking in a mirror. Thus, as I read my work, I expected to see and hear myself, not someone else.

Yet my situation as a foreign language learner and writer is unquestionably different from a second language situation with a second language learner and writer. I was simply writing mini travel essays, not studying in a degree program, taking rigorous humanities and social and natural sciences in Italian, and competing with Italian native speakers writing research papers, exams, and dissertations. With these pressures and challenges, more ESL writers may be more willing to trade some of their voice for accuracy, idiomaticity, and increased language learning. If I as a tutor had made the equivalent changes in the essay of an ESL student in the writing center, would she also feel as if I had appropriated it? Probably not—if she had expressed the desire to sound as native as possible, if she had participated in making the changes, and if I had done my best to explain why particular expressions were ungrammatical or unidiomatic. What had contributed to my sense of appropriation was not only my satisfaction with sounding nonnative, but also my not understanding the reasons for my teacher's changes and my lack of participation and control in making them.

Avoiding Appropriation

We can identify from these discussions the situational factors that can contribute to avoiding appropriation in tutoring ESL students in the writing center. When and how are we more likely to avoid appropriation? Paralleling the discussion of the continuum of second and first language writing features, appropriation should also be discussed in terms of probabilities and of gradations on a continuum of tutor and writer control and directiveness, as Straub recommends,[12] and not in terms of absolutes. It is not always clear—to a tutor or even to an outside observer such as a researcher—when appropriation has taken place, except possibly when a writer thinks and feels at a gut level that it has. If the notion of "appropriation" is applied in a judgmental fashion every time a tutor suggests changing an expression on an ESL student's paper and replacing it with a more idiomatic one—a labeling that Reid calls a "myth of appropriation,"[13] it will cause unnecessary tutor anxiety, paralysis, and guilt and the term will ultimately lose its meaning.

To avoid appropriation, then, tutors should strive to do the following:

1. Accord the ESL writer authority.   We are more likely to avoid appropriation if we accord ESL students authority as fluent, proficient speakers of, and writers in their own native languages and advanced speakers and writers in English who may know more about the rules of English syntax, grammar, and usage than we do. When we compare their proficiency in English with ours in our L2, we can gain an appreciation and admiration for their amazing achievements. By respecting their authority as bilingual speakers and writers, as knowledgeable students of their disciplines, and as cultural informants about their own native languages and cultures, we are less likely to assume control of their texts and impose our Ideal ones.

2. Work on higher-order concerns (HOCs) before lower-order concerns (LOCs).   We are more likely to avoid appropriating language and voice if we adhere to the principle of higher-order concerns versus lower-order concerns recommended by Donald McAndrew and Thomas Reigstad.[14] The assignment, focus, argument, development, and organization are usually more important than expression unless some language clarifications and corrections are needed simply in order to understand whether the student has followed the assignment and to understand her points. In the case of language completely obscuring argument, the level of language would be considered a higher-order and global concern. Otherwise, there is no point in working carefully and slowly to reformulate language that should not or probably will not appear in the next draft because the student needs to refocus or revise her entire argument.

3. Address expressed needs.   We are more likely to avoid appropriation when students, especially more advanced students and English learners, tell us that they want their writing to sound as much like that of native English speakers as possible. We can endlessly debate whether ESL writers *should* feel they should sound like native speakers rather than themselves, but the fact is, many do, especially advanced undergraduates and graduates, faculty, and visiting scholars; the feedback and pressure they receive from their professors, their supervisors, their dissertation advisors, and their journal editors convinces them that they need to feel this way.

As Kathy Lyons, one of the University of Iowa writing center tutors, noted, "When you factor in what's at stake for these more advanced students (opportunities for publication, the need to write a defendable thesis, jobs), it seems wrongheaded to resist their desire to gain mastery over American writing styles. . . . In resisting the request of an ESL student to help with learning the 'American way' or simply the 'standard English' way of expression something, we might be doing a great disservice, though with the best of intentions. We should be prepared to do what's in the student's best interest and to allow her to learn what she feels is important to her own professional and/or educational advancement if that is what she is asking us to do."

However, shouldn't we work to convince the gatekeepers in graduate and professional schools and in academic departments and on editorial boards that second language writers will probably always write with an accent? We should support the efforts the field of second language writing has made, such as the Conference on College Composition and Communication's resolution[15] to educate teachers about the length of the second language writing acquisition process and how, according to Virginia Collier, it takes at least seven years to acquire an academic vocabulary.[16] (See Chapter 4 for more about this.) However, until teachers and other gatekeepers are sufficiently educated and become more tolerant of accents and nonnative features in writing, some ESL students will ask to be taught how a native English speaker would say what they suspect they are saying awkwardly. Such requests might put pressure on a hands-off tutor into taking what I have called a more assimilationist stance, so that the student's writing will blend better into the linguistic mainstream of American Academic English.[17]

YiYun Li, a Chinese English bilingual writing center tutor at the University of Iowa, creative writer published in *The New Yorker*, and former microbiologist, is similar to Lyons when it comes to responding to students' expressed needs. Her perspective as an ESL writer who has both tutored and been tutored is especially valuable. "As an ESL student myself, I understand that students really hope to learn the most correct English from our tutors. I remember in our writing center class last year, we talked about whether we should want our students to write like Americans. The concern was that they would love their uniqueness. But a lot of times, this uniqueness is just what makes them uncomfortable about their own writings. For myself, I usually ask my readers to point out all things that sound unusual for a native speaker. Some of them I know I have put in intentionally to give the writing a little foreign-ness, but with others, I just don't know *the right ways*, and I always feel happy to learn how to say them right."

Writer-tutors like YiYun would want tutors to point out instances of inadvertent or intentional poetry in their writing so they can decide whether they want to leave them in their texts or reformulate them. Such writers want control over when they are sounding foreign or even, ironically, when they are sounding inappropriately colloquial—for example, when they are using the word *stuff* incorrectly or overusing it to try to sound like native English speakers. If their writing contains foreign features, they want to know it is because of a conscious decision on their part, not an accident or a result of not knowing an expression or idiom. In this case, the ESL writer paradoxically has control over the tutoring situation even when it seems that the tutor has more control over the writer's language. What might seem like appropriation to an outsider unfamiliar with the expressed needs of the writer is actually a balanced tutorial interaction.

If tutors are not sure how unique or how much like native English speakers their students want to sound, they should ask them rather than guess. They should have a frank discussion of the pros and cons of leaning toward either pole. Such meta-discourse—communicating about how to communicate—is probably the most significant way to avoid appropriation. For confusing passages, tutors can generate with the student's help two or three options that vary in idiomaticity, style, or register and ask have the student to choose among them, as in the previous options for revising Satomi's sentence.

4. Select particular passages to work on.   We are more likely to avoid appropriation if we prioritize and select passages from a student's writing to revise. Because there may not be time in one tutoring session and because it could be cognitively overwhelming for both tutor and student to reformulate all nonnative constructions, a few should be chosen, particularly:

- global problems that interfere with meaning, as Muriel Harris and Tony Silva recommend[18] (See also Chapters 6 and 7.)
- nonidiomatic passages about which the student expresses concern
- features that are ungrammatical rather than just nonidiomatic

5. Ask writers to participate in reformulation decisions.   We are more likely to avoid appropriation if students actively participate in the reformulation and revision process and more importantly, in the meta-discourse about the process. According to the Interaction Hypothesis, such participation is said to increase the chance that language learning takes place, as Jennifer Ritter points out.[19] Even if ESL students request a reformulation of their paper, when a tutor revises *for* them rather than *with* them, it is possible that that tutor crosses the line, as Molly Wingate says,[20] into appropriating the students' texts. University of Iowa tutor LuAnn Dvorak tells students who pressure her to change all incorrect or nonidiomatic features that they will not learn if she fixes everything for them; there is just too much new language in new contexts, she explains, for them to process in too little time and with too little participation on their part.

One common way for the student to participate is to read her own paper aloud and stop or put a check mark when she thinks a passage does not communicate well because it is ungrammatical, unnatural, or both. The tutor might stop her when he does not understand a passage to ask her if she can explain it. Another way for the student to participate more is for tutors to participate less, thus balancing the interaction. To establish this balance, we need to monitor the ways in which we are participating. Megan Knight, another University of Iowa writing center tutor, tries to limit herself to asking ESL students questions and mirroring what they have said.

6. Use speaking-into-writing strategies.   We are more likely to avoid appropriation if we use speaking-into-writing techniques that utilize the student's direct spoken language. This helps to capture and preserve his voice. Marilyn Abildskov, a former University of Iowa tutor and now a creative writing professor, says that "Tell me more" is the best question tutors can ask to elicit both participation and content for writing and to reflect the writer's voice. "Tell-me-more" questions about expression cause the student to clarify her intended meaning and often result in language that is clearer and more idiomatic than what is on the page. Working from reading aloud and from speaking in order to rephrase written passages is what University of Iowa tutor John Winzenburg calls the "outside-in approach." In contrast, "the inside-out approach," he says, is when the ESL writer is concentrating on how she thinks she should write rather than on what she is trying to say. By having the student verbalize and converse to find and revise written language, University of Iowa tutor Jen Ryan says she ensures that the voice on the page is not an English voice or, for example, a Chinese voice, but the student's voice.

7. Explain the recommended changes.   We are more likely to avoid appropriation if we offer brief explanations for why the student's passage is faulty and why our recommended changes are better, rather than just writing or typing them on the page. If the feature is based on a rule and the tutor can explain the rule, then this provides an opportunity for learning and carries over to the next writing rather than just repairing that one expression. For example, I would tell Satomi that the words "own _____" are preceded by a possessive adjective: *my own car, one's own name*. Why this word or expression and not that? Why should we say two chemicals "competed" with another to bond with a third chemical rather than "contended" with one another? Look up both words in the dictionary together to learn the connotations and contexts. Why this verb form and not another? Why a gerund rather than an infinitive in the second reformulation of Satomi's sentence? The changed construction has fewer words, is more economical and streamlined, and is easier to process, even though the infinitive in the original sentence was not ungrammatical. If a tutor doesn't know the explanation, then rather than invent one, it is best to look it up together in a grammar book or ask the tutors sitting next to you. We don't have to have an explanation for every change we suggest; indeed, students may not want or need them, and there may not be enough time for them, but "this is the way we say it in English" should not be our explanation for every change or replacement.

8. Try to assess language learning. We are more likely to avoid appropriation if the student learns new language or more about using language from the interaction and reformulation. It is difficult to determine whether learning has taken place because writing centers do not test, and they often don't see the same students regularly enough to monitor their learning. Yet, tutors who find themselves correcting and explaining the same features week after week should be aware that the student is possibly not participating enough in the exchange or the explanations are not communicated well. (See Chapter 2.)

9. Avoid misrepresenting the student's language level on the page. We are more likely to avoid appropriation if our recommended changes and the resulting reformulation do not project a level of language proficiency and sophistication that is inaccurate. Intermediate ESL students should not come across as advanced on a paper after a few trips to the writing center. Ethical issues are involved in misrepresenting the student's language level to outside audiences of teachers and other gatekeepers. Such misrepresentation is unfair not only to these audiences, but to the students themselves. What if I submitted my teacher's revision of "Un Viaggio a Venezia" to an Italian program and was admitted on the basis of my supposed ability to manipulate the language, but then could not understand my courses and professors? When readers of reformulated essays compare them to the students' in-class writing and speaking, they may feel betrayed by both the students and the writing center. (See Chapter 10.)

10. Consider the type of writing. We are more likely to avoid appropriation if we gauge the purpose, genre, and type of writing we are working on with the student. Informal writing, narratives, and reader-responses may benefit more from nonidiomaticity and features of the student's unique voice; formal essays, abstracts, proposals, and dissertations may benefit less. For example, if Satomi writes in a personal essay that her hometown is "abundant of green," we might let it go and not comment about it at all. Or we might compliment her on her poetic phrasing, but at the same time mention that native English speakers might say "abundantly green" or "very green." But if Satomi writes "abundant of green" to describe a land mass in a formal geography paper, we would more likely point out the lack of idiomaticity and offer the previous options. These decisions—whether to point out such instances and whether and how to change them, even in personal writing—should be negotiated with the student.

A Ten-Step Program?

Must all ten conditions be met and all the strategies implemented within a tutoring session in order to avoid appropriation? Some of these conditions and strategies are undoubtedly more significant than others. Responding to the writer's expressed needs and feelings (#3), ensuring the writer's participation (#5), and not misrepresenting the writer's second language proficiency level (#9) are probably the most important criteria and advice for avoiding appropriation, although not necessarily in that order. Most important, periodic meta-communication and perception-checking about whether and how to reformulate will work to help tutors avoid taking control over ESL students' texts and voices. Just as the travelers in my Italian essay negotiated and compromised but still met their needs and goals, so should tutors and ESL writers.

Notes

1. Cohen (1985).
2. Brannon and Knoblauch (1998).
3. Brannon and Knoblauch, 213.
4. Sommers, (1982).
5. Straub (1996).
6. Caposella (1996).
7. Gillespie and Lerner (2000).
8. Powers, (1993).
9. Reid, (1994). 273–92.
10. Matsuda and Silva (1999).
11. Leki (1992).
12. Straub, 225.
13. Reid, 290.
14. McAndrew and Reigstad, 42.
15. CCCC Statement on Second Language Writers, *www/ncte.org/cccc/positions/lang2*.
16. Collier (1987).
17. Severino, 190.

18. Harris and Silva (1993).

19. Ritter, 104.

20. Wingate, 9.

Works Cited

Brannon, Lil, and Cy Knoblauch. 1998. "On Students' Rights to Their Own Texts: A Model of Teacher Response." In *Harcourt Brace Guide to Peer Tutoring,* edited by Toni-Lee Capossela, 213–22. Fort Worth, TX: Harcourt Brace.

CCCC Statement on Second Language Writers, *www.ncte.org/positions/lang2.shtml.*

Capossela, Toni-Lee. 1998. *The Harcourt Brace Guide to Peer Tutoring.* Fort Worth, TX: Harcourt Brace.

Cohen, Andrew. 1985. "Reformulation: Another Way to Get Feedback." *Writing Lab Newsletter* 10 (2): 6–10.

Collier, Virginia. 1987. "Age and Rate of Acquisition of Second Language for Academic Purposes." *TESOL Quarterly* 21 (4): 617–41.

Gillespie, Paula, and Neal Lerner. 2000. *The Allyn and Bacon Guide to Peer Tutoring.* Boston: Allyn and Bacon.

Harris, Muriel, and Tony Silva. 1993. "Tutoring ESL Students: Issues and Options." *College Composition and Communication* 44 (4): 525–37.

Leki, Ilona. 1992. *Understanding ESL Writers.* Portsmouth, NH: Boynton/Cook.

Matsuda, Paul Kei, and Tony Silva. 1999. "Cross-cultural Composition: Mediated Integration of U.S. and International Students." *Composition Studies* 27(1): 15–30.

McAndrew, Donald A., and Thomas J. Reigstad. 2001. *Tutoring Writing: A Practical Guide for Conferences.* Portsmouth, NH: Boynton/Cook.

Powers, Judith. 1993. "Rethinking Writing Center Conferencing Strategies for the ESL Writer." *Writing Center Journal* 13 (2): 39–47.

Reid, Joy. 1994. "Responding to ESL Students' Texts: The Mytho of Appropriation." *TESOL Quarterly* 28 (2): 273–92.

Ritter, Jennifer. 2002. "Recent Developments in Assisting ESL Writers." In *A Tutor's Guide: Helping Writers One to One,* edited by Ben Rafoth, 102–10. Portsmouth, NH: Boynton/Cook.

Severino, Carol. 1998. "The Political Implications of Response to Second Language Writing." *Adult ESL: Politics, Pedagogy and Participation in Classroom and Community Programs,* edited by Trudy Smoke, 185–208. Mahwah, NJ: Lawrence Erlbaum.

Sommers, Nancy. 1982. "Responding to Student Writing." *College Composition and Communication* 33 (2): 148–56.

Straub, Richard. 1996. "The Concept of Control in Teacher Response: Defining the Varieties of 'Directive' and 'Facilitative' Commentary." *College Composition and Communication* 47 (2): 223–51.

Wingate, Molly. 2002. "What Line? I Didn't See Any Line." *A Tutor's Guide: Helping Writers One to One,* edited by Ben Rafoth, 9–16. Portsmouth, NH: Boynton/Cook.

6

"Earth Aches by Midnight"

*Helping ESL Writers Clarify Their Intended Meaning**

Amy Jo Minett

In 1993, I joined the Peace Corps and went to Hungary to teach English. And just as the commercials promise, it was a time of adventure: I stomped grapes during a harvest festival, got lost in a Transylvanian blizzard, and fell off bicycles on muddy village roads. But looking back, most vivid to me now is how I struggled to learn the language, to express myself and to make my meaning clear. It was a challenge shared every day by learners of other languages all around the world.

A story to illustrate this challenge was told to us by our Hungarian teachers. One newly arrived volunteer sat down to eat with her homestay family: they didn't speak English, nor she Hungarian, yet. Wanting to be gracious, she tried to ask what the main course—a delicious meat dish—was. Once she got her question across (through pointing, upturned palms, and a wondering tone), her homestay father smiled with delight. He lacked the vocabulary but knew the sound the animal made. "Ruff ruff," he replied proudly. The volunteer dropped her fork. "Ruff ruff?" she asked, a little fearful. "Ruff ruff!" repeated the father, and the rest of the family chimed in. "Ruff ruff!" The volunteer hesitated, then picked up her fork and went bravely on to eat her supper. Only later did it turn out—during an elementary lesson on "what do the animals say" (the duckie, the chicken, the cow, etc.)—that in Hungarian, the pig says, "Ruff ruff!"

In this story, the volunteer leaped to what seemed a logical conclusion (same sound, even if, in Hungary, a different animal makes it). Similarly, when we struggle to understand an ESL writer's text, it is tempting to leap to conclusions about the meaning the writer wants to convey. This chapter helps

---

* For his many research insights and invaluable guidance with this chapter, I am indebted to Dr. Dan Tannacito of Indiana University of Pennsylvania.

avoid this pitfall, first, by helping you, the tutor, understand *why* you might not understand. You might ask the following questions.

- Has the writer tangled the syntax, as in this typical example: *But most of people feel not natural that making small talk with strangers in my country*?

- Or has the writer used sudden, strange words? One of my students once wrote, in a lovely if confusing instance, "I do not want to know the earth ache."

- Or did the writer compose whole paragraphs of seemingly unconnected ideas, or save the thesis statement until the very end? Baffling though such texts sometimes are, in this chapter, you'll also find strategies that you can use to help English as a second language (ESL) writers clarify just what it is they want to say (and it's hard enough in a first language, right?).

First, though, let's explore *why* you may not understand an ESL writer's intended meaning. Then we'll look at how you can help clarify meaning at four levels: essay, paragraph, sentence, and word.

Clarifying the Essay's Main Idea

In 1966, Robert Kaplan published an article that dramatically changed how we understand ESL writers' texts. In it, Kaplan says that logic is not universal but culture-specific, and it's reflected in the patterns we use to organize texts in our first languages.[1] He arrives at this conclusion after studying hundreds of ESL student essays and identifying different types of development. While English essays are often linear (e.g., stating claims explicitly and then supporting those claims with evidence), essays written by Asian students may be much less direct and even withhold the thesis statement until the very end. In my experience, too, Russian, Polish, and Hungarian writers frequently hold off stating their main points until the last page—believing it creates more suspense for the reader—which is how they were taught to write. The problem, however, is that if you are accustomed to reading texts developed according to the conventional rhetorical patterns of academic English, the effects of *other* ways of structuring essays (be it Spanish, Russian, or Chinese) can cloud your understanding of an ESL writer's meaning.

Here's one rather startling example from the Budapest center in which I tutored. Magda, a Polish writer of a history paper, almost *seemed* supportive of the Nazis in the Holocaust, right up until the last paragraph, when she finally spun around and lamented the tragedy (in which members of her own family had died). When the somewhat anxious tutor asked why she had waited until the very end to make her position clear, Magda cried, "Because that's how I'd write it in Polish! It sounds best this way. Readers in Polish would *know* I wasn't siding with the Nazis!" The U.S. tutor, on the other hand, accustomed to a different pattern of essay development, was quite understandably misled by the writer's rhetorical choice of saving her thesis until the very end. Another reader may not even have finished reading, which would have been unfortunate, as the reader would have missed the writer's main point.

If you feel that cultural differences in text organization are affecting your understanding of an ESL writer's intended meaning, you might spend some time talking directly with the writer about contrastive rhetoric. In Magda's case, the tutor asked her how arguments were typically organized in Polish, and then they explored together how essays are usually structured in English. In this way, Magda came to understand how cultural differences might shape a particular reader's understanding of the intended meaning—in this example, an U.S. reader with U.S. expectations of essay structure—and she understood what changes she needed to make to meet those expectations. For instance, her conclusion, with some tinkering, became her introduction, which made her intended meaning quite clear (and poignantly so). Equally important, as Ilona Leki says, open discussion of contrastive rhetoric can produce in ESL writers "instant enlightenment about their writing in English, as students suddenly become conscious of the implicit assumptions behind the way they construct written ideas and behind the way English does."[2] Helen Fox, too, believes in talking directly with ESL writers about cultural differences in "communication styles" so that they can better understand the audience for whom they're writing, especially professors in U.S. universities who expect writing to be "so explicit and precise that they can follow the argument without any effort at all."[3] Perhaps most important such discussion also helps make clear how English conventions (and audience expectations) are, as Kaplan said, no better or worse than other conventions.[4] They're just different.[5] Finally, the writers' stories will be fascinating and may further put writers at ease as they become aware of what backgrounds and traditions they bring to the writing conference, and why they're not always understood.

Clarifying Paragraphs

Not only essay structure, but paragraph development, too, differs in other cultures and can blur our understanding of an ESL writer's meaning. Paragraphs might seem flip-flopped to us, as ESL writers often state the main point of the paragraph in the last sentence (as opposed to the first). John Hinds concludes that—while English writing is typically reader-friendly in its directness and clarity—Japanese writing, in contrast, is *writer*-friendly, and it's mainly the reader's job to determine the writer's intention.[6] He describes how Japanese authors like "to give dark hints and to leave them behind nuances" and how Japanese readers "anticipate with pleasure the opportunities that such writing offers them to savor this kind of 'mystification' of language."[7]

Part of this "mystification" comes from the different use of connectors like *however* or *in contrast*. While in English, we are taught to use these connectors to guide the reader explicitly through our logic (and through the ideas in our paragraphs: can you find all the connectors in this chapter so far? Have you even noticed them as you read?), in Japanese and other languages, these "landmarks" may be absent or at least more subtle, thereby demanding the reader be more active and work harder to understand the writer's meaning.[8] For someone who is used to reader-friendly English, understanding the meaning in such texts may feel like driving in a strange city without street signs or a road map. We want the writer to tell us exactly where to go. We want coherence and cohesion.

One strategy you can use to help ESL writers whose paragraphs aren't coherent (and whose meaning is therefore unclear) is called *topical structure analysis* (but don't be put off by the name. The strategy is easy.).[9] With it, writers are able to look at both global coherence (what the whole text is about) and local cohesion (how sentences "build meaning" by connecting to each other and to the text as a whole).[10]

In its simplest form, topical structure analysis works like this. Start by asking ESL writers to find sentence topics (what the sentence is about) in individual sentences. I might offer a sentence of my own, such as "<u>Writing poetry</u> is like meditation to me." Writers should underline "writing poetry" as the topic.

Next, ask them to find and underline the sentence topics in whole paragraphs and then discuss the relationship between the topics and the paragraph, and the paragraph and the whole essay. In so doing, writers should discover (1) different ways that sentence topics build meaning, and (2) that the reader's ability to understand the meaning depends in part on how the topics in the paragraph progress.[11] Here are examples I've used to help writers understand.

1. Parallel Progression:

    "<u>Writing</u> is often a struggle. <u>It</u> can also be a joy. <u>Writing poetry</u>, for example, feels like meditation to me."

Here the writer can see that the meaning of the underlined topics (writing, it, writing poetry) is the same. The main idea of the paragraph (writing) remains absolutely clear to the reader (though too much progression of this type may lead to monotony).

2. Sequential Progression:

    "<u>My room</u> is undoubtedly the messiest in the house. <u>Books and papers</u> are scattered everywhere. <u>My clothes</u> lie about in sad piles. <u>Anyone entering</u> does so at their own risk. <u>My brother</u>, for instance, last week tripped on a bean-bag chair and broke his foot."

In this example, the topics are all different (my room, books and papers, my clothes, anyone entering, my brother), though the meaning usually comes from the previous sentence. Clearly, too much development of this type can disorient the reader, a point which ESL writers quickly come to understand when they see how, as in this example, the writer goes off on one dizzying tangent after another and sentence topics continually shift and change.[12]

3. Extended Parallel Progression:

> "My room is undoubtedly the messiest in the house. Books and papers are scattered everywhere. My clothes lie about in sad piles. My room is a disaster."

Here we find the last sentence returning neatly to the first topic (my room, books and papers, my clothes, my room). In this way, the main idea is developed in detail but then restated again directly, which helps the reader understand the main focus of the passage. The paragraph is clear and coherent.

Once ESL writers get the hang of finding and analyzing progressions in sentence topics, you can ask them to "test" how coherent their own writing is by diagramming *their* underlined sentence topics, like this:

Parallel Progression

1. Writing
2. It
3. Writing poetry

Sequential Progression

1. My room
   2. Books and papers
      3. My clothes
         4   Anyone entering
            5. My brother

Extended Parallel Progression

1. My room
   2. Books and papers
      3. My clothes
4. My room

With the topics diagrammed this way, ESL writers can better see the relationships and coherence (or lack thereof) between sentences, paragraphs, and the main idea of the paper.[13] They can then revise so that the topics of their sentences build the intended meaning consistently and coherently throughout the paragraph. As a final "check" of coherence, Ann Johns recommends students write a one-sentence summary of paragraphs, which becomes more difficult if coherence is lacking and the sentence topics are constantly changing.[14]

This might also be a good time for you and the writer to discuss cohesion, or how sentences build meaning by connecting to each other. For this purpose, I always keep a handy list of common connectors (like *however*, *nevertheless*, *in addition*) over my desk to yank down and share with ESL writers who might need to make explicit the logical links that may be missing between sentences. Many college writing texts include such lists, Eli Hinkel notes, and ESL students especially need to understand what they mean, when and how to use them, and how vital they are when writing for college classes.[15] It's one more way you, the tutor, can help ESL writers clarify their intended meanings.

Clarifying Sentences

Focus on Form

So far, we've seen how cultural differences in essay and paragraph organization might obscure an ESL writer's intended meaning. Sometimes, however, single sentences are difficult to understand. To help the writer in this case, you might try a strategy from second language research called "focus on form."[16]

Interestingly, "focus on form" works best during a writing conference in which you and the writer still mainly concentrate on "higher order concerns." Don McAndrew and Tom Reigstad spell out these concerns nicely as being "central to the meaning and communication of the piece" like "matters of thesis and focus, development, structure and voice."[17] However, during such a conference, if you just *occasionally* direct the writer's attention to problems with language that obscure meaning, you can help the writer more clearly express herself, provided she is developmentally ready, that is, provided the writer has enough background knowledge about the meaning and use of the language form (see Chapters 2 and 5). For instance, can the writer use negatives correctly? Is the word choice accurate? Are verb tenses in control? In most cases, we can probably safely assume that ESL college writers are developmentally ready. Furthermore, if you as tutor help ESL writers notice their existing language problems, then you are actually engaging their developmentally sharpened language processing mechanisms, which help the writer break into the new language system like spies cracking a code.[18] In short, you are helping writers extract the form, which they can then map to meaning and function.[19]

Here's an example (to clarify my own meaning). If a writer has made a mistake and you don't understand the text, try repeating the unclear sentence back to the writer, perhaps in the form of a question, but with the mistake corrected. If the writer has written "I study by midnight," you could ask, "You study *until* midnight? Or *around* midnight? *At* midnight?" which might be enough to help the writer notice the problem with the preposition and how the meaning changes with each choice (unless he is too tired, having been up all night). Or, if we return to the example provided at the beginning of this chapter, "I do not want to know the earth ache," you might ask, "Earth ache? Hmmm. . . . Well, ache means hurt. Does the earth hurt in some way? Are you writing about environmental problems?" If the writer shakes her head, you might volunteer more suggestions. "Do you not want to experience an 'ear' ache? Or do you mean an earthquake, like what they have in California and Japan?" (The answer, by the way, was earthquake, which the writer most definitely did not want to experience.)

This technique is simple and useful, but we shouldn't forget that writers will benefit most from only the *occasional* focus on form, and on just one or two problems at a time.[20] For the most part, higher order concerns probably should remain just that—a higher priority.

This is probably also a good time to bring up the issue of appropriating a writer's text, which, as a trained writing center tutor, you might be worried about after reading the previous example (see Chapter 5). After all, we don't want to take over the writer's work, and volunteering words might seem like too much help. With ESL writers, however, we might need to rethink our approach to the conference. Joy Reid believes we have responsibilities as "cultural informant[s]" to our students.[21] I would add that we may also have—to some extent, at least—responsibilities to them as language resources. When we offer the writer a number of choices related to meaning (earth hurts? earache? earthquake?), it's still the writer's choice in the end to decide which word (and which meaning) he wants to convey. We might even see this as one way meaning is negotiated between tutor and writer, and second language research suggests quite strongly that negotiated meaning (1) facilitates learning, and (2) leads to better writing (and therefore, probably a clearer expression of meaning).[22]

How Much Help, and When?

If we take the view that you, the tutor, and the ESL writer will together negotiate the intended meaning as a part of clarifying what the writer wants to say, then it's also important to know how much help to give, and when. Some experts suggest that as tutor (and therefore, probably a more capable user of English), you can best help ESL writers work at their potential level of ability by offering help only so long as it's needed, and then withdrawing your help as soon as writers "show signs of self-control" and the ability to go it alone.[23] So, if Vlado, a Bulgarian writer, comes to me, here's what I'd do to help him express his meaning more clearly.

First, I'd ask Valdo to read his paper silently and, on his own, underline and correct the errors he can find (in the meantime, I'd drink a coffee, file papers, maybe hum a little). When he says, "Ready, Amy," I would sit beside him and together we would discuss the corrected errors, which might go like this:

"Yes, good, that's right: you were *bored* by Tolstoy, not *boring*, though it's too bad you weren't *interested* in the novel, because I think *War and Peace* is a very *interesting* book."

If he missed an error that obscures meaning, I might point to the sentence and look puzzled, or ask him, "Hmmm . . . is there anything wrong *here*?" If Vlado is still unable to see the problem, I would offer more direct help by pointing this time to the phrase or word and asking again: "What—about—here?" If Vlado is still unsure, I would target the problem directly: "Look at the verb tense here. 'I had been lived in Moscow for one year when I read Tolstoy.' Now, I know you don't live in Moscow now, because we're in Budapest. What's wrong with the verb tense?" If necessary, I will give the correct answer and explain the grammar rule, or we'll look it up together, but I will first offer help in ever more explicit and guided forms. Vlado will need my help only so long as he doesn't notice the error, or notices it but can't correct, or corrects just with specific pointing. Over time, however, he should rely less and less on my guidance, until finally he has consistent control over the problem structure, be it verb tense, word form, or something else.[24]

Interactional Cues

In the previous example, you may have noticed how my puzzled look communicated to Vlado that there was some kind of problem with the sentence. I might also have frowned, grinned, stroked my chin, or widened my eyes. What you didn't see were Vlado's facial expressions and the other signals he gave me that showed when he was struggling with something and when he was about to solve a problem by himself. Amy Snyder Ohta calls these "interactional cues," and she presents quite convincing research that shows that, as tutor, you can help the writer the most when you pick up on and respond to these often very subtle signals, for that's when the writer is most developmentally ready to listen, and learn.[25] In other words, you can read these cues to know when it's time to help clarify writers' intended meanings, and when they are probably on the verge of clarifying it for themselves. Here are some things you should listen for before jumping in.

- rising or falling tones of voice
  "The verb tense is past . . . present? I had lived . . . I have had . . . lived?"
  When the voice goes up at the end in question form, the writer is ready for help. If the voice doesn't go up at the end, the writer is still thinking, so don't jump in yet. Wait for more signals.

- restarts of sentences
  "The author, the author pre . . . per . . . , the author persites, presits, *persists*!"
  Re-starts indicate the writer is still working out the problem, so wait.

- rates of speech
  If the writer is speaking quickly, she is probably still at work on figuring out the best solution. When the rate slows down, you should get ready to offer help.[26]

These are just a few examples. As tutor, you too can learn to interpret the writer's many differing cues, especially if you meet with the same writer regularly. And one last point here: It's also important to remember that ESL writers frequently need more wait time after questions or when they are working out problems for themselves, so don't be afraid of longer silences. One way or another—by sigh or tone—the writer will let you know when he is ready for your intervention.

Clarifying Words

Lastly, a few words about words. Hinkel discusses an important survey in which U.S. college faculty describe ESL papers as too often "vague and confusing," precisely because the writer may lack the necessary vocabulary to clarify their intended meaning.[27] You can, therefore, also help ESL writers by talking about certain words that can help clarify meanings dramatically. Hinkel describes the following as top priorities for ESL writers:

- qualifying hedges like *apparently, probably, ostensibly, seems, perhaps, most likely*
- modal verbs like *may, might, should, could, can*[28]

In both cases, using these words can soften the writer's rhetoric considerably. Just listen to the difference in meaning between these two sentences:

> Raising tuition will lower student enrollment.
>
> Raising tuition will most likely lower student enrollment (we can't be sure it will, can we?).

You should also be prepared to encourage ESL writers to avoid vague nouns like *society, people, world*, or the vaguest of all perhaps, *truth*. My Hungarian students loved to use the phrases "to tell the truth" and "to be honest," which they had learned and were (justifiably) proud of. In most college writing, however, these phrases can be problematic. Helping ESL writers build their academic vocabularies this way can not only help clarify their intended meaning, it can also relieve some of the anxiety and frustration they feel when they get their papers back all marked up in red ink.

This chapter has explored why you may not always understand an ESL writer's meaning, and it has offered the following strategies that you can use to help writers clarify just what it is they want to say.

- You can explore with writers how they learned to write and what's expected at U.S. universities.
- You can help them analyze how coherent their paragraphs are.
- You can guide them through rough sentences and help them choose clearer words.

Through my work tutoring ESL writers, I've learned that in Egypt, babies are welcomed into the world by a party on the seventh day. In Taiwan, the number four is unlucky (it rhymes with the word for *death*). What challenging work, I say. And how rewarding.

Notes

1. Kaplan, 12.
2. Leki, 138.
3. Fox, 114.
4. Kaplan, 12.
5. For more on contrastive rhetoric, see Panetta (2001) or Connor (1996).
6. Hinds, 65.
7. Suzuki, quoted in Hinds, 66.
8. Hinds, 67.
9. This idea comes from Connor and Farmer (1990), 126–39. Connor and Farmer draw on the work of Finnish linguist Liisa Lautamatti.
10. Connor and Farmer, 127.
11. Connor and Farmer, 128–33.
12. Connor and Farmer, 130.
13. Connor and Farmer, 130.
14. Johns, 256.
15. Hinkel, 144.
16. Long in Doughty, 259–84.
17. McAndrew and Reigstad, 42.
18. Doughty, 276.
19. Doughty, 265.
20. Doughty, 290.
21. Reid, 218.
22. See, for instance, Goldstein and Conrad (1990).
23. Aljaafreh and Lantolf, 466–68.
24. Modeled after Aljaafreh and Lantolf, 469–71.
25. Ohta, 52.
26. Ohta, 62–77.
27. Hinkel, 52.
28. Hinkel, 247–50.

Works Cited

Aljaafreh, Ali, and James P. Lantolf. 1994. "Negative Feedback as Regulation and Second Language Learning in the Zone of Proximal Development." *The Modern Language Journal* 78 (iv): 465–83.

Connor, Ulla. 1996. *Contrastive Rhetoric: Cross-cultural Aspects of Second-Language Writing*. Cambridge: Cambridge University Press.

Connor, Ulla, and Mary Farmer. 1990. "The Teaching of Topical Structure Analysis as a Revision Strategy for ESL Writers." In *Second Language Writing: Research*

Insights for the Classroom, edited by B. Kroll, 126–39. New York: Cambridge University Press.

Doughty, Catherine. 2003. "Instructed SLA: Constraints, Compensations, and Enhancements." In *The Handbook of Second Language Acquisition*, edited by C. Doughty and M. Long, 256–310. Oxford: Blackwell.

Fox, Helen. 1994. *Listening to the World: Cultural Issues in Academic Writing*. Urbana, IL: NCTE.

Goldstein, Lynn M., and Susan M. Conrad. 1990. "Student Input and Negotiation of Meaning in ESL Writing Conferences." *TESOL Quarterly* 24 (3): 443–60.

Hinds, John. 2001. "Reader Versus Writer Responsibility: A New Typology." In *Landmark Essays on ESL Writing*, edited by T. Silva and P. K. Matsuda, 63–73. Mahwah, NJ: Lawrence Erlbaum.

Hinkel, Eli. 2002. *Second Language Writers' Text*. Mahwah, NJ: Lawrence Erlbaum.

Johns, Ann M. 1986. "Coherence and Academic Writing: Some Definitions and Suggestions for Teaching." *TESOL Quarterly* 20 (2): 247–65.

Kaplan, Robert B. 2001. "Cultural Thought Patterns in Intercultural Education." In *Landmark Essays on ESL Writing*, edited by T. Silva and P. K. Matsuda, 11–26. Mahwah, NJ: Lawrence Erlbaum.

Leki, Ilona. 1991. "Twenty–Five Years of Contrastive Rhetoric: Text Analysis and Writing Pedagogies." *TESOL Quarterly* 25 (1): 123–43.

McAndrew, Donald A., and Thomas J. Reigstad. 2001. *Tutoring Writing: A Practical Guide for Conferences*. Portsmouth, NH: Boynton/Cook.

Ohta, Amy Snyder. 2000. "Rethinking Interaction in SLA: Developmentally Appropriate Assistance in the Zone of Proximal Development and the Acquisition of L2 Grammar." In *Sociocultural Theory and Second Language Learning*, edited by J. P. Lantolf, 51–78. Oxford: Oxford University Press.

Panetta, Clayann Gilliam. 2001. *Contrastive Rhetoric Revisited and Redefined*. Mahwah, NJ: Lawrence Erlbaum.

Reid, Joy. 2001. "The Myths of Appropriation." In *Landmark Essays on ESL Writing*, edited by T. Silva and P. K. Matsuda, 209–24. Mahwah, NJ: Lawrence Erlbaum.

7

Looking at the Whole Text

Jennifer Staben and Kathryn Dempsey Nordhaus

A student walks into the writing center, sits down in the chair next to you, and pulls out a paper, announcing, "I'm a terrible writer. Can you read this and tell me if I did it right?" Another student comes in, sits down, pushes a paper across the table, and says, "My English is terrible. Can you help me with it?" Both students offer their papers with an unvoiced disclaimer: my work isn't necessarily a reflection of my *self* or my *knowledge*. Both students offer their papers with an unvoiced request: please help me without judging me. But only one of these students speaks English as a second language (ESL). Can you guess which?

The answer lies at the heart of these students' requests. The native English-speaking (NES) student has invited you to critique her writing—the whole text; whereas, the ESL student has invited you to critique his English—the language. Although this may at first appear to be a small semantic difference, it's a difference that looms large in a writing conference. The goals of most writing centers today reflect Stephen North's "idea" of writing centers: "to produce better writers, not better writing."[1] To achieve this goal, tutors are trained to look beyond the language—to look at the text as a whole; to look at the text within the context for which it is created; and to look at the writer's relationship with the text and with the audience the text will reach.

That's the goal, but it can be a challenge to meet it when working with an ESL writer. Language difficulties may be the first things you notice as you read a given piece or the student's main reason for coming to the writing center in the first place. Some ESL writers use the request "Can you check my grammar?" in a very general sense to mean "Could you look this over for me?" Others definitely mean what they say; they want help with their English and they ask for it directly.

Because writing centers strive to be student-centered, writing conferences with ESL students often make tutors feel that they are faced with a difficult choice: comply with the ESL students' invitations to focus on grammar and

71

other surface errors or ignore the ESL students' requests and focus on the whole text. Opting for the former often leaves tutors feeling like traitors to the cause: they have helped contribute to the perpetuation of the image of a writing center as a "skills center, a fix-it shop."[2] Opting for the latter, however, sometimes leaves tutors feeling more like *intruders* than *collaborators*; they have forced their way into students' ideas—their minds—without an invitation and may be rebuffed for doing so.

What's a tutor to do? Though there are no easy solutions to the tension this apparent dichotomy produces, the dichotomy itself is false: Tutoring objectives are rarely as simple as *either* grammar *or* the whole text. Yet even in situations when the student and the text pull you toward focusing solely on grammar, we believe that you should resist. ESL students, like their NES counterparts, have much to gain from looking at the whole text.

Some Background

At first glance, the texts produced by ESL students and by NES students sometimes appear strikingly similar. For instance, you may notice that both ESL and NES students produce texts with a number of surface errors: misplaced or missing punctuation, shifting verb tenses, or spelling errors. Regardless of these similarities in the *texts*, you sense that the needs of the *writers* are different, calling for different strategies in a writing conference. Both research and anecdotal evidence support tutor intuition: ESL students' needs *are* unique. Before reviewing some strategies you might apply to meet these unique needs, it might be helpful to look at some of the ways ESL writers differ from NES writers.

Many students, regardless of their linguistic background, are challenged by the demands of writing for academic audiences. Academic writing requires students to analyze and synthesize materials from a variety of sources, to draw conclusions based on these analyses, and to support these conclusions with objective and subjective evidence. For many NES students, meeting the expectations of the academy involves adopting a new writing style, while relying on the fundamental skills—language, grammar, and structure—they learned in elementary and secondary school. For ESL students, the challenges of writing in the academy include all of these issues and more.

Why is this so? First, ESL students face the obvious challenge of language. Although NES students may struggle with punctuation or spelling, for instance, most can rely on their native ear to make appropriate word choices and cogent sentence patterns. ESL students, on the other hand, lack that ear. Although they may have extensive English vocabularies and a sound understanding of grammar rules—knowledge often superior, in fact, to their NES counterparts—they often lack the ability to hear their mistakes, to sense when something is not quite right. ESL students often turn to writing center tutors to provide the ear they lack. Tutors, in turn, are often overwhelmed by the linguistic issues on the page. As Muriel Harris and Tony Silva remind us, "To the untrained tutor's eye what is most immediately noticeable is that a draft written by an ESL student looks so different."[3] In short, the surface errors, when combined with ESL students' hesitancy, accent, and uncertainty, can make language issues appear more urgent than they really are—to tutors and students alike. In response to this perceived urgency, tutors tend to try to provide the ear with a sentence-level approach; they assume the role of linguistic informant on issues like sentence structure and word choice.

Sentence-level assistance can be helpful to ESL students (see Chapter 8 for helpful strategies). These strategies can help put to rest some of the students' linguistic anxiety. However, it does not address far less obvious challenges ESL students face as academic writers: cultural differences. Although tutors and ESL students are aware that cultural differences exist, both tend to underestimate their significance and scope.

Most writing tasks in U.S. colleges and universities are based on cultural conceptions about clear writing and effective argumentation—ideas that may not be shared by ESL writers. In *Listening to the World*, Helen Fox tells countless stories about how upper-level undergraduate and graduate students, proficient and sometimes professional writers in their first language, struggle less with the linguistic aspects of English and more with U.S. academic expectations of how writers construct arguments, utilize outside authorities, and even incorporate personal experience and viewpoints into academic texts. Fox suggests that this struggle is not simply an issue of adopting a different style of writing; U.S. academic texts require students to assume different ways of viewing the world and their place in it.[4] For example, when Fan Shen discusses his own experiences as a writer moving from a Chinese academic culture to a U.S. context, he explains that making the transition was not as simple as switching pronouns—from *we* to *I*. Instead, he had to learn to create a more individualistic stance for himself when he wrote essays in his English composition course—one that not only used the pronoun *I* but valued it in a different way.[5]

Contrastive rhetoric studies suggest that "not simply rhetorical style but also purpose, task, topic, and audience are culturally informed."[6] Therefore, it seems clear that ESL writers may need resources—"cultural informants"—to help them understand the assumptions and expectations of a U.S. academic audience, assumptions that are not usually directly addressed on the assignment sheet.

This role of cultural informant would appear ideal for writing center tutors. It is, in many respects, an extension of the facilitator role tutors play with NES writers—questioning the students about the needs of the audience and how the text might change to meet those needs. However, with ESL students, this role as facilitator is complicated by issues of language and culture. With many NES students, tutors can use Socratic questioning techniques to elicit knowledge from the writer that the writer may, in turn, incorporate into the text. In contrast, for ESL students as well as inexperienced NES writers, these same techniques may be doomed to fail because no amount of Socratic questioning can elicit language or cultural knowledge the writer doesn't possess. These writers need an informant to provide them with the background they need to successfully negotiate these new writing contexts.

To complicate matters further, even the experts don't always agree on how a tutor can successfully perform the informant role. For instance, Susan Blau and John Hall believe that interweaving discussions of language and vocabulary throughout a tutoring session may be more appropriate with ESL writers, particularly those with less experience writing in English.[7] On the other hand, Carol Severino,[8] as well as Muriel Harris and Tony Silva,[9] maintain that higher order, rhetorical concerns should still come before linguistic concerns. Similarly, many tutor guidebooks, such as *The Allyn & Bacon Guide to Peer Tutoring*, encourage writers to put higher-order concerns first.[10]

Acting as a cultural informant about U.S. academic expectations—rhetorical or otherwise—can be difficult because no matter what the background of the ESL writer, language is a concern. Some ESL students have spent time in high school or middle school in the United States. These students may seem to be familiar with aspects of American culture and language, everything from customs to idioms, but they often lack knowledge of U.S. academic culture, just like any inexperienced writer. And because English is not their first language, students may assume that good writing is the same as correct writing. At the same time, other ESL students may become overwhelmed while trying to write because of the cognitive complexity of the task.[11] These are the students who often literally cannot see the forest for the trees: They are so focused on the language—on trying to wrestle their complicated thoughts onto paper using language abilities that are not yet sufficient to the task—that they may not realize that the change in language and in culture necessitates a different approach to communicating those thoughts to others. For both sets of students, language concerns can overshadow rhetorical ones and important conversations about academic culture and expectations may not take place. This is where you and the whole text come in.

What to Do

Tutoring sessions are as individual as fingerprints: they may progress along a familiar pattern only to whorl suddenly off into new and unexpected directions. Therefore, we don't have specific procedures for you to follow, but instead, we offer some thoughts, some suggestions, and even some anecdotes, in the hope that one or more of these approaches may suggest approach(es) appropriate for your ESL tutoring situations.

Talk Before Text

One of the strengths of writing center conferences has always been the interactive talk between tutor and tutee. Although questions may not work in the same way with ESL writers as they do when working with an NES student, we would argue that they can still play a critical role in the writing center conference. One of the ways to incorporate questioning into conferences with ESL students is to talk with the writer *before* turning your attention to the text.

- One way to get the conversation started is to focus first on the assignment. Most tutors have had the experience of discovering at the end of the session that a student had completely misinterpreted the instructor's directions. Oftentimes, this misinterpretation is caused by cultural differences. We forget that the writing assignment itself is cultural; although students might understand the individual words, they still may not have a clear idea of what the instructor expects. Read the assignment. Ask the writer questions about his understanding of the expectations of the assignment and how he tried to meet them. Telling students that they are on the wrong track can be difficult. However, it is even more difficult to tell a student that fact after you've spent forty minutes helping him generate and develop ideas that don't adequately address the assignment. (See Chapter 3.)

- Another way to start a conversation before turning to the text is to ask ESL writers what they chose to write about in response to the assignment and why they chose it as the subject for their papers. The simple request "Tell me what your paper is about" can be useful when working with any ESL writer, but it is especially productive when working with students who are inexperienced writers in both English and their native language. These discussions can help both of you notice differences between what the writer has told you and what is on the page—differences you and the writer can negotiate together.

- A third way to start a conversation is to focus on the writer's process. The text is typically what draws writers into the writing center. As a result, we often focus on the product, neglecting the process altogether. To learn about the writer's process, tutors can ask students questions, such as: "When did you start writing this paper?" "Have you written other drafts?" "Have you received feedback yet?" "What do you plan to do next?" "How can I help you achieve your goals?"

After surveying research on the composing processes of ESL and NES writers, Harris and Silva suggest that:

> ESL writers might find it helpful to stretch out the composing process: (1) to include more work on planning—to generate ideas, text structure, and language—so as to make the actual writing more manageable; (2) to have . . . ESL students write in stages, e.g., focusing on content and organization in one draft and focusing on linguistic concerns in another subsequent draft; and (3) to separate their treatments of revising (rhetorical) and editing (linguistic) and provide realistic strategies for each, strategies that do not rely on intuitions ESL writers may not have.[12]

With these ideas in mind, we believe that asking preliminary questions—about the assignment, the topic, and the writer's process—is a critical step in the writing conference. This approach can help you and the writer prioritize and set goals and it's also a good way to focus the student's attention (and yours) on larger textual issues from the very beginning.

Read (and Read, and Read) with Purpose

If your opening questions are meant to help the writer focus on the text as a whole, we believe it is important for your session to begin with the text as a whole as well. That is, in most situations we recommend reading through the entire essay with your tutee before focusing on the parts. Though there are situations where going through an ESL writer's text paragraph by paragraph or line by line is appropriate, it is difficult to talk about issues of overall focus and organization after reading only the first paragraph or two, especially when the writer may be using different rhetorical strategies than the ones you are used to. It is definitely easier to see patterns—whether they are related to focus, organization, or language—if you approach the paper as a whole first.

Similarly, many tutors find it useful to read through the piece once to get an overall impression, with either tutor or student reading out loud (see Chapter 4 for more on reading student papers aloud), and then to go through the paper a second time to talk specifically about issues both the tutor and the tutee notice. Since some writers, both NES and ESL, write their way to their main points, this strategy can help tutors address issues of thesis and focus much more effectively. Also, if you notice that a writer consistently employs the same unexpected organizational strategy throughout his paper—putting the main point at the end of each paragraph, for instance—then you can more easily explore the idea that this is something the writer is controlling, which can then be negotiated, as opposed to something that is out of control.

Be Direct, Not Directive

When working with ESL writers, and indeed all writers, we believe it is important to understand the difference between being *direct* and being *directive*. That is, you need to negotiate the fine line between being direct by giving the students information they don't have—about academic expectations, essay conventions, or grammar constructions—and being directive by telling writers what they *have to do* with that information for a specific essay. If you simply tell ESL writers that they need to put a thesis sentence near the beginning of the essay or that they should organize their research paper in a certain manner, you are not helping them understand what you likely know instinctively—the web of assumptions and conventions that shape different writing genres. It is an understanding of genre(s) that will help the ESL writer negotiate future writing tasks. One of the best ways to help the student understand is to explore the topic together, through interactive discussions where you and the student share your questions and information.

Another reason to be direct, rather than directive, is that it presents opportunities for you to learn. In a truly interactive conference, both the tutor *and* the student learn from each other. When you are directive, the student is forced to be a follower. For example, several years ago a graduate student from Japan was working with an undergraduate tutor on an essay for a course in second language acquisition (SLA). The tutor responded to the writer's use of the terms *production* and *utterance* in regards to language learning by informing her that these were not the expected ways to say these concepts in English. The writer tried to explain that these words were established vocabulary in the field of SLA, but the undergraduate tutor ignored this explanation. The tutor was unable to see the graduate student across the table from her, an individual with specialized knowledge; instead, she saw an ESL student with a vocabulary problem. Rather than asking the writer why she had used these words and then creating a space in the session for discussion and negotiation, the tutor was directive, closed off conversation on this issue, and lost the chance to learn about an unfamiliar discourse community.

As you work with each student on overall textual issues, it is important to remember that while there frequently is logic behind the choices a writer has made in a given draft, it is difficult to understand those choices without asking the writer. To put it simply, being direct means understanding when questions might *not* be the most effective way to generate knowledge, but being directive means forgetting about times when they *are*.

Tell . . . and Show

Although questioning is the cornerstone of effective writing conferences, it isn't always enough. When ESL writers seem to be struggling with an assignment—an assessment based either on what they say when talking to you about it or on what you see happening on the page—don't hesitate to address this issue directly. Telling students what a teacher might expect to see in response to the assignment and what you as a reader see happening in their papers is one way to begin the discussion.

For example, a situation we see frequently in our writing center is ESL students struggling in their second composition course—a course that focuses on writing about literary texts. Though some instructors spend a great deal of class time helping students develop strategies for analyzing works of poetry, fiction, and nonfiction, others assume all students will understand their request to "write a literary analysis of _____." Students often come to our center with long summaries of the works they're supposed to analyze and are unsure what the difference is between what they've done and what they're supposed to do. In these kinds of situations, modeling can be a very useful strategy. Try to walk the writer through your own thinking and writing processes if you were given an assignment similar to this. The key is to focus on the *process* you would go through and not the *content* you would generate. Our sessions with these students often involve going back to the story or poem itself and modeling how to look for patterns or themes and then how to move from these things to thinking about them on paper and in an essay format. In doing this, it is important to keep the session interactive. Unfortunately, it can be all too easy to tell writers what to do rather than to relate to writers what they need to know to perform the task successfully themselves.

Don't underestimate the power of textual models. Sometimes instructors will give students a sample paper or two to help them understand the assignment. In other cases, they will provide these samples if the student writer requests them. If the writer has a sample paper, you might consider going through it with him. Models are only helpful, however, if students notice the parts they are supposed to (see Chapter 2). By asking questions and pointing out textual features, you can help the writer understand the qualities and conventions of the model that she might want to utilize. For instance, if the sample is a

- narrative essay containing rich description and dialogue, you might ask the student to consider why the author used these techniques and why the instructor might value them.

- book review paper from a history class, and the writer keeps the summary of the book separate from the critique, you might highlight and discuss this separation with your tutee.

You can help an ESL writer see a sample as more than a rigid formula to follow. Instead, you can show how it is a specific articulation of larger principles underlying a type of academic writing. These principles may affect every aspect of the piece—from topic selection and organization to the language itself.

Respond as a Reader

Sometimes tutors can get so caught up in what is different about what they see on the page that they forget the most important role they can play with ESL writers—as a reader. Just like their NES counterparts, ESL writers often need feedback on what they're saying—their ideas—and not just on how they're saying it. Some tutors, especially tutors working with older or more experienced students, hesitate to discuss ideas. Sometimes this hesitance stems from a fear of appearing uninformed and thus undermining their credibility or authority. But often tutors shy away from discussing ideas because they don't want to offend the student; grammar is safe, neutral territory, while ideas are potentially explosive minefields filled with personal beliefs and values. (For ideas on how to be a better reader of ESL students' papers, see Chapter 4.)

There are ways to approach ideas with respect and sensitivity:

- Share your own ideas.
- Point out places where an essay suggests connections to your own life or experiences.
- Point out ideas that make you think—or make you think differently.
- Highlight places that are unclear to you; ask the writer to expand her ideas by providing examples or anecdotes that help clarify her thoughts to you.
- Play devil's advocate—help the writer see other sides to his ideas.
- Identify places where the writer could strengthen her argument by acknowledging other opinions, or where she could diffuse counterarguments by addressing them directly.

This is one area where the Socratic approach can serve you particularly well. When you're questioning someone gently and are truly interested in what he has to say, it's hard to offend. In fact, the opposite is often the case. Many writers come to the center blocked by their discomfort with the language. Your questions can reassure the writers that although their language skills may not be perfect, they aren't interfering with their ideas, and their ideas are interesting to others.

Use the Power of Paper

It is vital to know when talk is not enough. The spoken word can be extremely powerful, but when placed on a page, writers tend to think of it as permanent. This perceived permanence of words on paper can be intimidating to writers and can especially block ESL writers. However, there are ways you can harness the power of paper to work for the student's benefit.

One of the simplest things you can do for students is to serve as a scribe. Some ESL students speak fluently and have no problems expressing themselves verbally because they don't stop to translate what they want to say; they simply say it. But when it comes to putting words to a page, the process might be more arduous. (The reverse is true as well: Some students who are not fluent speakers of English may be fluent writers if they learned English mainly through writing and reading.) Initially, they might write their thoughts in their first language and then translate their ideas. Or, they may write their thoughts in a mixture of both languages, planning to "smooth it out" later. Both of these processes can affect the product. If you suspect this may be the case, or if you are having a difficult time understanding what the student has written, ask the student for clarification and write down his response. Although this is a common practice for working with NES writers, it may be even more important for ESL writers who are balancing several complex cognitive tasks at once.

Another way you can use paper to the students' advantage is to get *away* from words. We regularly use outlines or lists with students in the writing center—ESL students should not be an exception. You might also consider graphically illustrating the various elements of a piece of written work (introduction, body, conclusion), showing the relative size and importance of each, along with some notations about what kinds of things might be included in each element. These illustrations can be used to represent both the forms the writer is trying to learn and the actual structure of the writer's text. (See Chapter 3 for ideas about creating graphic models.)

The benefits of this strategy are many. These techniques can help loosen up a blocked ESL student by turning her attention from a troublesome sentence or paragraph and helping her see, literally, the big picture. ESL writers who are visual learners may benefit more from these pictures than their explanations. In addition, by creating a picture, you are giving the ESL writer something physical to take with her—an additional reference she can consult as she seeks to revise her writing.

Complicating Matters

In this chapter, we have tried to review one of the challenges you're likely to face when working with ESL students in the writing center: finding ways to pull students' attention toward higher-order concerns such as focus, development, and organization, and away from lower-order concerns such as grammar or word choice. It sounds like a simple goal, but it's an extremely complex issue with no easy solutions. To a certain extent, it is this complexity that presented the two of us with unexpected challenges when writing this chapter. We kept getting sidetracked by "what-ifs." We'd like to share some of these "what-ifs" here because they're the kind of complications you may encounter.

What if the student is a repeat customer and has already been to the writing center several times to work on content and organization? What if the student is insistent about working on language only? What if one of the myriad factors that *can* affect the focus of a writing conference (the time pressure of last-minute visits to the writing center, a tutor's awareness of a particular instructor's grading criteria, and/or a tutor's desire to be helpful and student-focused) *does* affect the conference? In these situations, it's important for tutors to remember several things:

- You don't have to choose between substance and grammar. Though the goal is to focus as much as possible on higher-order concerns, it doesn't necessarily mean you should focus on these concerns to the exclusion of everything else.

- Most students' time is at a premium: they are students, employees, daughters, fathers, friends, and so on. They need to use their time wisely; if they truly have little need for additional discussion of higher-order concerns (as in the case of the repeat customer), their time—and yours—may be best spent on issues of language. (See Chapter 8 for strategies; see Chapter 14 for a broader perspective on discussing issues of language.) However, even these situations provide room for *conversation*. Try to find out why the student made the language choice she made, and you may discover entirely new areas to discuss. A misplaced comma might lead to a discussion of how punctuation is used in Spanish—or Hindi or Korean—and how that might affect the relationship between author, audience, and text.

- Your students' needs are driven by the situation in which they find themselves. Our preference to focus on higher-order concerns stems largely from our desire to address the majority of our students' needs. We support a community college with a significant ESL population from a wide range of backgrounds—from international students with multiple degrees earned in their native countries to immigrant students who are inexperienced writers in English and their native language—but the majority of our ESL students are inexperienced writers in any language, and they tend to benefit most from assistance with larger textual issues. In environments with upper-level undergraduate or graduate ESL students, it might be more appropriate to shift the balance toward the middle ground between text and language—or shift more toward language.

Finally, remember the cornerstone upon which every writing center is founded: trust. *You* are working with the student. *You* are there to read his body language, her inflection, his facial expressions, her motivation and intensity. You must trust yourself and your instincts to make the right decision based on the information you have at the time. You must trust the student's knowledge of his own needs and priorities. And ultimately, you must trust in the validity of the ultimate goal of the kind of writing center Stephen North describes—a place for the "creation of a continuous dialectic that is, finally, its own end."[13] Sometimes this requires a pragmatic approach. You may need to cut a deal now to lure the students back later, so the conversation can continue and the real growth can begin.

One final note: Tutors need to be engaged in another type of conversation as well, and that is the one that all professionals have with the research in their field. We offer some suggestions for further readings we think you will find helpful and interesting:

Leki, Ilona. 1991. "Twenty-Five Years of Contrastive Rhetoric: Text Analysis and Writing Pedagogies." *TESOL Quarterly* 25 (1): 123–43.

In this article, Leki gives a useful overview of the various strands of contrastive rhetoric research and discusses a number of ways that contrastive rhetoric can and should influence writing instruction.

Spack, Ruth. 1997. "The Acquisition of Academic Literacy in a Second Language: A Longitudinal Case Study." *Written Communication* 14 (1): 3–62.

In this research study, Spack follows Yuko, an undergraduate international student from Japan, over the course of three years and explores how Yuko develops academic literacy in English. Spack's research not only highlights the complex-ities involved in this undertaking but also suggests ways that teachers and tutors can assist international students as they negotiate this process.

Tucker, Amy. 1995. *Decoding ESL: International Students in the American College Classroom.* Portsmouth, NH: Boynton/Cook.

In this book, Tucker examines how the cultures and cultural rhetorics of both students and teachers influence what happens in the college writing classroom. She demonstrates through multiple examples the need for teachers to learn to "read" and "reread" their students, an idea that is equally important for tutors.

If your writing center does not already have a professional library for tutors, these readings and others cited in this book would make a great start. They will draw you into a conversation you will want to continue for a long time.

Notes

1. North, 76.
2. North, 73.
3. Harris and Silva, 526.
4. Fox (1994).
5. Shen (1989).
6. Leki, 133.
7. Blau and Hall, 23–44.
8. Severino, IV.2.3.
9. Harris and Silva, 531.
10. Gillespie and Lerner, 126.
11. Leki, 107.
12. Harris and Silva, 529.
13. North, 83.

Works Cited

Blau, Susan, and John Hall. 2002. "Guilt-Free Tutoring: Rethinking How We Tutor Non-Native-English-Speaking Students." *The Writing Center Journal* 23 (1): 23–44.

Fox, Helen. 1994. *Listening to the World: Cultural Issues in Academic Writing.* Urbana, IL: NCTE.

Gillespie, Paula, and Neal Lerner. 2004. *The Allyn & Bacon Guide to Peer Tutoring.* New York: Pearson/Longman.

Harris, Muriel, and Tony Silva. 1993. "Tutoring ESL Students: Issues and Options." *College Composition and Communication* 44 (4): 525–37.

Leki, Ilona. 1991. "Twenty-Five Years of Contrastive Rhetoric: Text Analysis and Writing Pedagogies." *TESOL Quarterly* 25 (1): 123–43.

————.1992. *Understanding ESL Writers: A Guide for Teachers.* Portsmouth, NH: Boynton/Cook.

North, Stephen M. 1984. "The Idea of a Writing Center." In *Landmark Essays on Writing Centers*, edited by C. Murphy and J. Law, 71–85. Davis, CA: Hermagoras Press.

Severino, Carol. 1998. "Serving ESL Students." In *The Writing Center Resource Manual*, edited by Bobbie Bayliss Silk, IV2.1–IV2.7. Emmitsburg, MD: IWCA.

Shen, Fan. 1989. "The Classroom and the Wider Culture: Identity as a Key to Learning English Composition." *College Composition and Communication* 40 (4): 459–66.

8

Editing Line by Line

Cynthia Linville

Judy greets Tang at the door of the writing center with a smile, and as they get started on their session, Judy asks Tang what she can help him with today. Tang replies, "My professor said my paper cannot pass because it has so many errors in it. I need to fix every one of them. Please help me so that I can pass!" Nearly every experienced tutor has faced a situation like this one. Tang's goals for the session are very clear: line-by-line editing until the paper is error-free. Judy is facing a dilemma because, after glancing at Tang's paper, she knows that even if she corrected every error for him, one session would not be enough time to effectively edit Tang's paper. The first task of a tutor in this situation, then, is to negotiate a more realistic goal with her student.

A collision of student goals and tutor goals during writing center sessions is not uncommon. Students are often focused on the short-term goal of earning a passing grade on the assignment at hand, while tutors are often focused on teaching the students portable skills that can be applied to any assignment. When faced with editing an English as a second language (ESL) writer's paper, the tutor is often at a loss to determine how skillful an ESL student might realistically become in editing his own errors, knowing that he lacks the *native ear* for the language. Frustrated tutors are often tempted either to give the student too much help with errors or to give none at all, directing the student's attention to rhetorical issues instead. Most would agree that neither of these solutions is satisfactory. To help tutors with this dilemma, this chapter explores concrete strategies for providing appropriate and realistic help in editing ESL papers for errors, line by line.

Research has shown that college-level ESL students can and do learn to become proficient editors of their own texts when given the necessary instruction. For example, Dana Ferris conducted a semester-long study of ESL university freshmen and found that 28 out of 30 students were able to significantly reduce their errors over time as they practiced self-editing strategies.[1] When a student can learn what her most frequent errors are, and learn to recognize and correct her own mistakes, then she will be a proficient self-editor.

Convincing a student that learning to edit his own papers is both possible and necessary, however, is a difficult task for a tutor, a task that requires persistent and consistent effort. Despite the difficulty, I believe that teaching students to become effective self-editors is absolutely vital to fulfilling the writing center's mission of helping students become independent writers. The alternatives are unacceptable: providing a proofreading service, which creates the unhealthy dependency Carol Severino discusses in Chapter 5, or not providing the service at all.

Most tutors don't need to be convinced that teaching ESL students to self-edit is a worthwhile goal; they simply aren't sure how to go about it. Just as ESL students need to learn how to identify and correct errors, their tutors need to learn how to do so as well. This is more difficult than it seems because tutors will need resources beyond their native knowledge of English to carry out these tasks. When faced with a paper filled with grammatical and lexical mistakes, tutors need strategies for spotting *patterns* of recurring errors, pointing those patterns out to the student, and providing rules about how to correct those errors. In addition, tutors need to know which kinds of errors are most important to address. This chapter explores six types of major errors that ESL students and their tutors can correct together. While focusing on this limited set of errors will not enable students to produce error-free writing, this narrow focus will enable students to improve their writing. Most important, though, it provides a way to limit the focus in an ESL writer's paper to certain types of errors. I find it important to note, however, that a tutor is not a grammar teacher. His ability to help is limited, as Paula Gillespie explores in Chapter 11; and yet, a tutor must master some knowledge of grammar in order to understand the six types of errors (see Chapter 14 on the need for tutors to learn more about the structure of English). Sometimes a tutor will find it necessary to refer a student elsewhere for more instruction, as will be discussed later in this chapter.

Before examining these issues in more depth, a summary of goals discussed so far might be helpful.

Goals for the Student

Acknowledge the need to become a proficient self-editor.

Learn what his most frequent patterns of error are.

Learn how to recognize these errors.

Learn how to correct these errors.

Goals for the Tutor

Teach the student how to become a proficient self-editor.

Learn how to identify frequent patterns of error.

Learn how to correct (and teach students to correct) six major error types.

Learn when to refer students elsewhere for more instruction.

Error-Correction Research

Some researchers note that while proofreading is usually against writing center policy, many students request this service, and some tutors do provide it. In one study, the authors suggest that writing centers should consider lifting the ban against proofreading.[2] Research has shown, however, that direct error correction (crossing out errors and writing in corrections) does not prevent students from making the same errors in the next paper, nor does it seem to promote student learning.[3] In addition, scholars generally agree with writing center pioneer Steven North: the overarching purpose of writing center tutoring is to "intervene in and ultimately alter the composing process of the writer,"[4] that is, to *improve* students' writing skills toward the goal of making them independent writers. Accordingly, most writing centers have a policy against tutors acting as proofreaders. Teaching students to become self-editors, then, is the tutor's best alternative. At the same time, tutors will need to point out some types of errors that ESL students are not able to recognize on their own, as described in Chapter 2.

Dana Ferris has demonstrated a successful approach in teaching students to become effective self editors through: "(a) consciousness-raising about the importance of editing in general and of each particular student's areas of need; (b) training in recognizing major error types; (c) teaching students to find and correct their own errors."[5] ESL writing specialists agree that identifying errors should focus on those that are the most frequent, serious, and treatable.[6] Serious errors are usually defined as those that interfere with communication; treatable errors, those that students can most readily learn to self-correct.

Clearly some students will evidence serious errors not included in the six error types presented in this chapter. When *any* error is interfering with communication, it should be addressed. Tutors should be aware, however, that some language features, such as prepositions, articles, and precise word usage, can take many years to learn; thus while such errors may be serious, they may need to be handled differently than other errors. This will vary depending on the student's level and ability.

Six Error Types

Six error types that are treatable and are often frequent or serious in ESL college compositions follow:

1. subject-verb agreement
2. verb tense
3. verb form
4. singular/plural noun endings
5. word form
6. sentence structure

Subject-verb agreement errors occur when the subject does not agree with the verb in person or number. These errors can be as simple as *He* walk *every morning* or as complex as *Every teenager knows how to choose clothes that* flatters *her figure.*

Verb-tense errors occur when an incorrect time marker is used. For example: *I* was *working on my paper since 6:00 AM,* or *Even though this is my first day on the job, I have already found out that there* were *some difficult people here.*

Verb-form errors occur when a verb is incorrectly formed, as we see in the following sentences. *I* will driven *to the airport next week*, and *I* was cook *dinner last night when you called.*

Singular and plural errors often occur when there is confusion about which nouns are countable and which aren't. For example, *I have turned in all my* homeworks *this week*, and *I set up six more* desk *for the afternoon class.*

Word form errors occur when the wrong part of speech is chosen: *I'm happy to live in a* democracy *country*, and *I feel very* confusing *this morning.*

Sentence structure errors refer to a broad range of errors that occur for a variety of reasons: a word (often a *to be* verb) is left out; an extra word (often a duplicate subject) is added; word order is incorrect; or clauses that don't belong together are punctuated as one sentence. For errors like the following, asking the student for the intended meaning is key, as Minett explores in Chapter 6.

> As a result of lack of moral values being taught by parents and the reemphasis by school many children have little respect for authority.

Note that sentence structure errors often contain other types of errors within them.

While these six error types *are* rule-based and thus treatable, it is important to note that the rules behind these errors are more complex than tutors may first believe. To deal with these errors effectively, tutors often need to know a good deal more about the grammatical structure of English than they often do, and unless they can explain the errors clearly and accurately to their ESL writers, it is advisable that they avoid grammatical concepts with which they are not familiar. This will quickly become apparent in line-by-line editing sessions. In addition, there are exceptions to every rule, exceptions for which ESL students will demand explanations. Because of this, effective tutors will need to study, discuss, and even debate grammatical rules together before they can provide this kind of help to ESL writers.[7]

Tutor Resources

Successful tutoring sessions begin behind the scenes with the appropriate tutor resources and training. One resource every writing center needs is an ESL grammar handbook. If you can only choose one, I suggest Janet Lane and Ellen Lange's *Writing Clearly: An Editing Guide*.[8] A handbook and workbook combined, this text provides clear rules, strategies, and practice exercises help-ful to both students and tutors. In addition, the unit topics correspond to the errors discussed (with additional errors covered as well).

Writing Clearly is also a helpful resource in developing ESL grammar handouts for use in tutoring sessions.[9] A concise, clear resource sheet on *each* of the six major error types is needed in order to follow the suggested tutoring strategies presented in this chapter. I recommend that each resource sheet include an explanation of the error and the grammatical rule(s), several cor-rected examples of the error, and three to five uncorrected practice sentences.

Another valuable handout is a list of ESL resources available *outside* the writing center. There will be times when a tutor *cannot* be of help in line-by-line editing because the student does not yet have the level of language acqui-sition necessary for such a task. In those times, a referral to an ESL grammar class or intensive English program may prevent the student from leaving the writing center empty-handed. A list of interactive ESL grammar websites is also helpful.[10]

The handbook, grammar resource sheets, and referral sheet make it possi-ble for tutors to use the following strategies without any additional training; however, additional training and practice in ESL error-correction will help tutors gain more knowledge, feel more confident, and be more effective during tutoring sessions. Ask a tutor trainer for suggestions.

Tutoring Strategies

At the opening of this chapter, Judy is beginning a tutoring session with Tang, who has unrealistic goals for their hour together. Judy's first task is to negoti-ate a more realistic goal with Tang. She might begin by reflecting back and affirming his stated goal. "I understand that correcting the errors in this paper is very important to you, and we will certainly spend most of our time during this session focusing on your errors." Next, she might gently inform him that the goal of an error-free paper at the end of the hour is not possible, but let him know what is. "I do need to tell you, though, that we won't have time today to correct *all* of your errors, so we're going to focus on your most frequent and serious errors here. Is that OK with you?"

Tang might need time for this point to sink in. In rare cases, he may become angry, depressed, or difficult as he feels his hopes being dashed. It would be best for Judy to pause until Tang has understood this point. (Role-playing practice outside the session is useful for situations such as these. Tutors need practice maintaining calm confidence even when the negotiations go awry.) A reminder that the clock is ticking might be helpful in persuading a stu-dent to move ahead.

Before Judy begins examining Tang's paper, however, another step in the negotiation is needed. Judy needs to outline the procedure, especially if Judy and Tang have not edited together before. Judy might say, "I'm going to take a look at your paper and point out what some of your most serious errors are. Then we'll review the rules behind those errors and correct your paper together. Is that OK?" Once they are in agreement on the procedure, Judy is ready to begin looking for Tang's patterns of error, focusing on the six error types previously outlined.

A paragraph from Tang's paper might look something like the example here.

> Jackson applied for a job and was given an interview since he had all the necessary skills for the job; however he *does* [verb tense] not have the moral values *suck* as *respect other people or when not to use abusive language* [sentence structure]. So during Jackson's *interviewed* [word form], he interrupted and used foul language toward his interviewers, and *a as* result he did not get the job. However, with the *institute* [word form] of moral values as part of the school *academic* [singular/plural], *it will* [sentence structure] *improves* [verb form] or *built* [verb form] on to the moral values each student already *possessed* [verb tense].

After marking the errors as shown here, Judy might ask Tang to read the paragraph aloud, correcting any mistakes he sees.[11] Judy is quickly able to determine that words such as *suck* instead of *such* and the word order problem of *a as result* are typographical mistakes, but Tang is not able to correct any of his other errors. After glancing through the rest of his essay, Judy notices many more *word form* errors like these two, so she decides to focus on those first, marking them throughout the essay.

After Judy shows Tang his pattern of word form errors and reviews the Word Form Grammar Resource Sheet with him, they are ready to begin editing Tang's paper together. Judy points to the first error, reads it aloud, and asks Tang, "How can we correct this?"

during Jackson's *interviewed*

This point in the session is frequently one of the most difficult for the tutor because she must suppress her urge to give too much help. I suggest that tutors put down their pencils and wait patiently and silently for the student to give a response, prompting the student only when he cannot offer an alternative on his own. This is quite difficult, but very necessary. It is important for tutors to remember that an unhealthy dependence on the tutor will be formed if the tutor is too willing to supply the correct answers (see Chapter 5 for more on this).

After a few moments of silence, Tang gives the answer *interviewing*, which of course is not quite right. Even still, Judy does not supply the correction. She directs Tang's attention back to the example and rule on the resource sheet and asks him to determine what part of speech the word should be (verb, noun, adjective, or adverb). On the second try, Tang gets it right: *interview*. Judy then asks Tang to write in the correction and double-checks to see that he wrote down his correct verbal answer. They proceed onward exactly this same way until all of the word form errors are successfully edited. If there is more time, Judy and Tang can move on to verb tense or verb form. After repeated sessions like these, the student can be led to recognize his own errors and correct many of them on his own. Editing sessions like the one portrayed here become the foundation on which students become proficient self-editors.

Granted, this method of editing is excruciatingly slow. In order to follow these suggestions, tutors will need to fight down their own sense of urgency. It is only natural to feel that too little is being accomplished in a session as slow-moving as this. Yet simply by marking a pattern of error and providing Tang with the information to correct those errors, Judy is providing a valuable service. By refraining from giving corrections, Judy affirms Tang's ownership of the paper, encouraging him to become a proficient self-editor. Tutors must be convinced of the benefits of this approach in order to implement these strategies. If a tutor is not sure that he *is* convinced, I suggest he discuss these ideas with a tutor trainer.

The scenario described here between Tang and Judy is a successful one. At times the session will be faster-moving because the student is already skilled at correcting his own errors once they are pointed out. But more frequently, a session can move even slower than the one described. A tutor might wonder how slow is too slow. What can a tutor do if, after waiting patiently between each guess and reviewing the rules several times, it becomes clear that the student is not able to correct her own work with the tutor's assistance? That is the time to bring out the ESL referral sheet and point the student toward a class or lab that can help her learn the skills she needs.

The tutor might say something like this, "It looks to me like you need to brush up on your English grammar before we can edit together. Here are some places where you can do that." Again, role-playing outside of the session can help tutors navigate difficult situations like this one. If the tutor is convinced that it would be unethical for him to correct the student's errors and that teaching ESL grammar exceeds his limitations, he will be confident in referring the student elsewhere. However, that doesn't mean the session has to end there. If the student is willing, the tutor can then refocus the session on rhetorical issues.

More often than not, however, tutors will find that their line-by-line editing sessions with students *are* successful. After the student has become aware of what his frequent patterns of error are, has learned the rules needed to correct those errors, and has become fairly proficient in correcting the errors his tutor marks for him, he is ready to begin finding errors on his own. An interim step toward that goal is for the tutor to be less direct in pointing out errors. In a future session between Judy and Tang, for example, Judy might say, "I see several word form errors in this paragraph. Can you find them?" If Tang has trouble finding them, Judy might say, "I see two on this line." If Tang still doesn't spot them, Judy could read that line out loud, exactly as it is written. Again, patient silence is needed while the student struggles to find the errors. Gradually, the student will become more proficient in finding his own errors; then he will be ready to learn how to proofread his own papers.

Clearly the student won't be able to proofread for every kind of error, so knowing her most frequent patterns of error is important. The tutor can ask the student to underline the types of words she has the most trouble with. For example, if the student has difficulty with subject-verb agreement, the tutor can ask the student to single-underline every subject and double-underline every verb, one paragraph at a time. This is something that can be practiced together during tutoring sessions until the student gains proficiency. Once the student has no trouble marking the frequent trouble spots in her paper, she is ready to start proofreading on her own, assisted by the grammar resource sheets she has already been working with. When a student reaches this stage of independence, her tutor should rejoice in the knowledge that she has played a big part in fulfilling the writing center's mission of helping students become proficient, independent writers.

Sample Word Form Grammar Resource Sheet

Explanation of the Error

Word form errors occur when the correct word is chosen but an incorrect *form* of the word is used. For example, in the sentence, *Young people can be* independence *in the U.S.A.,* the noun form is used instead of the adjective form. The sentence should read, *Young people can be* independent *in the U.S.A.*

Most words in English have different forms for different parts of speech, but not all words have all forms. For example:

noun	*verb*	*adjective*	*adverb*
independence	X	independent	independently
bath	bathe	bathing	X
confusion	confuse	confusing	confusingly

Some word forms look the same for different parts of speech. For instance, *anger* can be either a noun or a verb.

Some words have more than one form for the same part of speech. For example, *bored* and *boring* are both adjectives, but their meaning is different. *The student is bored* indicates that something outside the student is causing the boredom (such as the classroom lecture). *The student is boring* indicates that the student herself is causing the boredom (possibly by talking for too long).

Some word forms have a different meaning than expected. For instance, while *to intimate* is a verb form of *intimacy, to intimate* does not mean to become more intimate as might be expected. Instead it means to imply something, to hint at secret information. Consult a dictionary to be sure of word meanings.

Word endings often indicate part of speech. For example, words that end in *-ly* are usually adverbs. *Quickly*, *slowly*, and *happily* are all adverbs. Consult an ESL handbook or dictionary for more examples. Attentive reading is the best way to improve fluency with word forms.

Corrected Examples

The politician *emphasis* the need for more funding for education. (incorrect)

The politician *emphasized* the need for more funding for education. (correct)

In this example, the wrong part of speech is used.

My daughter *independences* daily. (incorrect)

My daughter *becomes more independent* daily. (correct)

Here, a nonexistent form is used.

I have two best *friendships*, Hung and Le. (incorrect)

I have two best *friends*, Hung and Le. (correct)

In this example, the correct part of speech (noun) was chosen. But *friend* has more than one noun form, and the wrong form was chosen.

Practice Sentences

I just finished *decoration* the house for Halloween.

I feel very *healthily* today.

Sue whispered *quiet*.

After reviewing my notes, I still feel *confusing*.

We helped raise funds to *beauty* our neighborhood.

Notes

1. Ferris (1995).

2. Olson, Moyer, and Falda (2002). Olson dissents from this view, however.

3. For a summary of error correction studies see Leki (1990) and Ferris (2003), chap. 3, 42–68.

4. North, 28.

5. Ferris (1995), 45.

6. For example see Harris and Silva (1993), and Ferris (1999).

7. An excellent comprehensive reference for such study is Celce-Murcia and Larsen-Freeman (1983).

8. Lane and Lange (1999).

9. Also useful are Master (1996) and *Longman Dictionary of American English* (2003).

10. I recommend these interactive grammar websites:

The ESL Quiz Center, *www.pacificnet.net/~sperling/quiz/#grammar*
The English Page, *www.englishpage.com/index.html*
Self-Study Grammar Quizzes, *http://a4esl.org/q/h/grammar.html*
For more links go to:
Ruth Vilmi's Links, *www.ruthvilmi.net/hut/LangHelp/Grammar/interactive.html*

11. This method is suggested by David Bartholomae (1980).

Works Cited

Bartholomae, David. 1980. "The Study of Error." *College Composition and Communication* 31 (3): 253–69.

Celce-Murcia, Marianne, and Diane Larsen-Freeman. 1983. *The Grammar Book: An ESL/EFL Teacher's Course*. Boston: Heinle and Heinle.

Ferris, Dana. 1995. "Can Advanced ESL Students Become Effective Self-Editors?" *CATESOL Journal* 8 (1): 41–62.

—————. 1999. "The Case for Grammar Correction in L2 Writing Classes: A Response to Truscott (1996)." *Journal of Second Language Writing* 8 (1): 1–11.

—————. 2003. *Response to Student Writing: Implications for Second Language Students*. Mahwah, NJ: Lawrence Erlbaum.

Harris, Muriel, and Tony Silva. 1993. "Tutoring ESL Students: Issues and Opinions." *College Composition and Communication* 44 (4): 525–37.

Lane, Janet, and Ellen Lange. 1999. *Writing Clearly: An Editing Guide*. Boston: Heinle and Heinle.

Leki, Ilona. 1990. "Coaching from the Margins: Issues in Written Response." In *Second Language Writing: Research Insights for the Classroom*, edited by Barbara Kroll, 57–68. New York: Cambridge University Press.

Longman Dictionary of American English. 2003. White Plains, NY: Longman.

Master, Peter. 1996. *Systems of English Grammar: An Introduction for Language Teachers*. Englewood Cliffs, NJ: Prentice-Hall.

North, Steven. 1984. "Writing Center Research: Testing Our Assumptions." In *Writing Centers: Theory and Administration*, edited by Gary Olson, 24–35. Urbana, IL: NCTE.

Olson, Jon, Dawn Moyer, and Adelia Falda. 2002. "Student-Centered Assessment Research in the Writing Center." In *Writing Center Research: Extending the Conversation*, edited by Paula Gillespie, Alice Gillam, Lady Falls Brown, and Byron Stay, 111–31. Mahwah, NJ: Lawrence Erlbaum.

9

Tutoring ESL Papers Online

Ben Rafoth

From a student perspective, online tutorials can be very convenient, whether they are based on instant messaging, discussion groups, bulletin boards, white boards, informational websites, or e-mail with attachments. They are quick and easy. But when the writer is not present and cannot answer questions to provide a sense of direction for the session, what should tutors respond to, where, and how often? What does experience tell us about what works and what doesn't? These are questions we faced when we began tutoring online several years ago with students from several undergraduate classes. The tutors in our writing center and I, the director, learned a number of important things about responding to the papers that English as a second language (ESL) and native speakers submitted. We learned that less is often more when it comes to writing comments, that focus and consistency are paramount, and that writers can misconstrue nondirectiveness. We also learned that how tutors read the writer's paper was crucial to the kinds of responses they wrote. This proved significant because tutors bring to each tutorial their own ways of reading and defining the task, and so training tutors to respond effectively begins with an awareness of the many ways one can read a paper. In this chapter, I look closely at a short sample of ESL writing and use it to illustrate some of the lessons we learned from our online experience.

The following is a key paragraph from one writer's paper. When submitting the paper, the writer asked the tutor for help with grammar and organization but offered little additional direction. While it is possible to infer something of what the writer is trying to say in this paragraph, doing so is a struggle and most readers would find it rather difficult to read the entire paper. The writer would benefit from a tutor who could make suggestions for improvement. But what suggestions should a tutor make? The paragraph consists of only sixty-seven words but poses a number of challenges, made especially difficult when the author is not available to clarify his intentions or guide the tutor's attention:

India and Nigeria are not democracy that share internal conflicts between diverse ethnics and religion groups. Two countries faced the same path of colonialism and created parliamentary democracy. At a time of independence, they were not ready to control over the country, since then they faced several difficulties to maintain the democracy. Their positions as democracy are not stable, moreover, the possibility to fail is likely today.

What exactly does the writer want to say? How would a passage like this be handled if the tutor were in a face-to-face session with the writer? What should the tutor look for when she reads this paragraph? How can the tutor be most helpful to this writer?

Reading Papers, Reading Responses

Before we continue on with this example, it is necessary to explain how our online writing center worked.[1] It was relatively simple, comparable to those many writing centers have adopted in recent years. To send a paper online, students first pasted a template of questions from our website into the top of their essay file and answered them. For example:

1.   Please tell us your name, course, instructor, and due date for the paper.
2.   What is the assignment? The more specific you can be, the better.
3.   Tell us *one or two* areas you would like us to help you with. Please be as specific as possible.

Then students sent an e-mail to our writing center with their essay files attached. We logged the incoming e-mails and forwarded them to tutors at home or in the writing center who read the attachments, wrote responses directly in the essay file, and sent them back to the students as attachments, always within 48 hours. As the writing center director, I received a copy of each response, which I then used to give feedback to the tutors and to evaluate the system. We also asked students to complete a brief survey and to participate in a follow-up interview about their online tutoring experience. Four of the students we interviewed were ESL writers, and we used their feedback and that of native speakers to improve the quality of tutors' responses.

Early on, it appeared that tutors were not as effective online as they were in face-to-face sessions. The biggest challenge seemed to come from ESL papers containing lots of language problems, long papers, and papers in which the writer offered little guidance or description of the assignment. The difficulty was apparent with the first batch of papers tutors responded to. Instead of targeting their feedback to a particular aspect of the assignment, as they were instructed to do in our initial training meetings, most tutors tended to insert a variety of comments along the way as they read the paper. The tendency was greatest when students made vague or incomplete requests for help, as they often did.[2] Tutors' comments were far-ranging, from questions about the author's intended meaning, to suggestions about relating the thesis statement to the rest of the paper, to reminders about a rule of punctuation or correction of an idiom, to praise for a well-chosen word or interesting idea. In other words, there was little focus to the feedback, just a lot of it inserted throughout the paper.[3]

One look at these responses and it was obvious that they were not in keeping with the more open-ended and collaborative quality of the face-to-face sessions we conducted in our center. Tutors began with a greeting to the writer and a brief self-introduction ("Hi ——————, I'm Marie, a tutor at the writing center, and I'll be reading your paper today.") and then delved into it. The outcome for many of the papers tutors worked on was a mix of questions, comments, suggestions, and corrections inserted into lines and paragraphs, usually in bold. Upon opening these files, one was struck not only by how much, but how all-over-the-map the feedback appeared to be.

There was no doubt that tutors had spent a great deal of time on the papers and took their responsibilities seriously. But why did tutors respond as they did? Why didn't the training they had received instructing them to focus responses on one or two areas sink in? Moreover, did online feedback have to be so lopsided, or could it become more focused and contained? One reason why tutors adopted this mode of responding, we learned from each other in our staff meetings, was that ESL papers usually presented them with many opportunities to give this type of feedback; the ESL writers who submitted papers often asked for help with grammar when they sent us their papers, and language problems were usually not hard to locate. We also learned that tutors believed that providing lots of feedback was the way to be most helpful to all students, not just ESL writers. The tutors' explanation for this was interesting: in lieu of the assistance they were accustomed to giving in face-to-face meetings—carrying on conversations, reading carefully, smiling, nodding, questioning, affirming, and so on—they felt that being helpful in online sessions meant pointing out lots of strengths and weaknesses and, in general, reacting often to the text. In other words, their sense of responding to writers as a communicative act was reshaped by the online environment. As one tutor remarked, "I want to show them I worked on their paper." With no writer to talk to, tutors saw the ball in their court, so to speak, and they worked conscientiously to scroll through each paragraph and make one comment after another. They usually chose to insert comments directly into the writer's text because they found it difficult or impossible to point to specific parts of the paper or to read more than one screen at a time. To illustrate, here is the writer's paragraph again, but this time with a tutor's comments, in brackets and italics.[4]

India and Nigeria are not democracy [*do you mean* democracies? democratic countries?] that share internal conflicts between [due to? *I'm a little confused* here] diverse ethnics [ethnic *is an adjective and doesn't take an* s] and religion [*the adjective form of* religion *is* religious, *and that's what you want to use before the noun* groups] groups. [*You need to begin this sentence with the article* the here] Two countries faced [*need the* here, too] same path of colonialism and created parliamentary democracy. [*I'm not that familiar with this part of history, so maybe I'm missing something, but . . . are you saying that colonialism created parliamentary democracy? If so, then you might want to explain how colonialism brought this form of government about. Just a thought.*] At a time of independence, they [*who was not ready?*] were not ready to control over [*you could omit the word* over, *or you could say* they were not ready to exercise control over] the country, [*you probably want to end the sentence here.*] since then they faced [*it's interesting to read about the link between present-day problems and past history—could you say more about this?*] several difficulties to maintain [*it's better to say* in maintaining] the democracy. Their positions as democracy [*the plural form is* democracies] are not stable, moreover, the possibility to fail is likely today.

Some writers might consider this to be a helpful response, as most of our tutors did. It appears to give the student the help with grammar and organization he asked for, reflects an inquiring tone, provides explanations, encourages the writer, shows frankness, and demonstrates a close and careful reading by the tutor. And yet, the sheer quantity of inserted comments is overwhelming to look at. The tutor gives no indication of priorities for what is most and least important, and the response takes for granted that helping the writer means addressing nearly every deviation from standard edited English.

Responses that provide lots of feedback to students run the risk of being too helpful, and it is a problem familiar to readers of writing center research. Too much help can involve appropriating the student's text, as Carol Severino discusses in Chapter 5, or overtaking the session and overwhelming the writer, as Molly Wingate writes about.[5] Except that in our case, we discovered the problem wasn't exactly too much help as not the right kind of help, because what eventually put tutors on the right track, after studying the feedback we received from writers and modifying our training, was not merely writing less but writing more selectively. This, in turn, depended on how tutors read the papers to begin with.

Within a few weeks, tutors had altered the ways they responded to all students' texts, including ESL papers in which language was a recurring problem. They were able to do this not by simply changing what they wrote in their feedback but by changing the way they read the papers. Recall that in Chapter 4 Matsuda and Cox, among others, describe three approaches readers can take to ESL texts: assimilationist, accommodationist, and separatist. When we apply this notion to tutors reading an ESL student's paper, we can see that with an assimilationist stance, the tutor reads the ESL writer's text with an eye toward some ideal form of nativelike writing and defines her task as one of making the flawed text conform to the flawless ideal. With an accommodationist stance, the tutor is more accepting of differences between native and ESL texts and tries to let the writer decide how nativelike he wants his text to become. Finally, with the separatist stance, the tutor reads multicultural differences in writing sympathetically and tries to help the ESL writer express her ideas clearly without regard to the rules of standardized form. These three approaches thus form a continuum of acceptance of differences, with the assimilationist approach being the least accepting, the separatist being the most, and the accommodationist falling somewhere in the middle.

The previous tutor's response reflects an assimilationist stance toward language differences, and this competed with her attempts to read for meaning. In terms of language, the tutor read the text against a type of ideal form that she thought a native speaker might write. While it's hard to know exactly what ideal form the tutor had in mind—and this is one of the problems with reading a text in this way—it might have been something like the following, a paragraph that most college-level instructors would consider generally clear, logical, and error-free.

> India and Nigeria are not entirely democratic countries; they also share similar internal conflicts due to their diverse ethnic and religious groups. The two countries faced a history of colonialism, which eventually led to the parliamentary democracies that govern these countries today. When the two states became independent of their colonial rulers, however, they were not ready to control their own countries. Ever since then, they have faced difficulties in maintaining democratic elements in their systems of government. As a result, their status today as democracies is not stable, and there is the likely possibility of failure.

When we compare this "ideal" form to the writer's original, the contrast is so great that the ideal becomes rather preposterous. No amount of diligence on the part of the ESL writer would produce the ideal text and no amount of expert tutoring could prepare him to write in this manner because the two texts emanate from such different sources, culturally and stylistically. Moreover, we cannot even be sure this is the meaning he intended for the paragraph. For this reason, it is fruitless to read this ESL writer's own text against a conjured ideal, and any response based on such a reading cannot be effective. It can only detract from tutoring strategies better suited to helping the writer build on his own ability level (see Tseng's discussion of Vygotsky's concept of zone of proximal development in Chapter 2).

A Revised Example

One can imagine, for example, how the feedback might have looked if the response had still attended to grammatical problems but refrained from comments pertaining to superficial surface forms. In the case of the ideal text, for instance, surface forms like the inclusion of definite articles serve more to improve smoothness and signal a polished academic register than to carry the burden of meaning. In other words, we can imagine a reading of the text that leaves surface problems alone while focusing on the writer's intended meaning, thus producing comments aimed at language problems involving unclear meaning.[6] This reflects an accommodationist or perhaps even a separatist stance on the part of the tutor, as the following example illustrates. Though the response still has some problems, as we will see, it says less but achieves more focus.

> India and Nigeria are not democracy that share internal conflicts between *[due to? I'm a little confused here]* diverse ethnics and religion groups. Two countries faced same path of colonialism and created parliamentary democracy. *[I'm not that familiar with this part of history, so maybe I'm missing something, but . . . are you saying that colonialism created parliamentary democracy? If so, then you might want to explain how colonialism brought this form of government about. Just a thought.]* At a time of independence, they *[who was not ready?]* were not ready to control over the country, *[you probably want to end the sentence here.]* since then they faced *[it's interesting to read about the link between present-day problems and past history— could you say more about this?]* several difficulties to maintain the democracy. Their position as democracy are not stable, moreover, the possibility to fail is likely today.

When comments about superficial forms unrelated to meaning are taken out, as in this example, what remains are two requests for clarification and elaboration of ideas: *I'm not that . . .* and *it's interesting to read . . .* and three comments about grammar and form:

1. Choice of preposition: *due to?*
2. Pronoun reference: *who was not ready?*
3. Sentence boundaries: *you probably want to end the sentence here*

The point here is that honoring an ESL writer's request to read and respond to a paper's grammar and organization can be accomplished by limiting the focus to problems that involve unclear meanings.[7] A writer's request for help with grammar cannot be construed as a license to make even part of the paper editorially flawless. As the hypothetical, ideal text illustrates, making an ESL text conform to standard edited English does not involve merely correcting its errors; it entails infusing it with ideas, supplanting its original voice with that of a particular but nonexistent native speaker's, and giving it the rhythms and turns of phrase of a distinct, native, and decidedly academic register.

What if we were to remove even those comments about prepositions, pronouns, and sentence boundaries? Would the effectiveness of the tutor's feedback be enhanced or diminished? Consider the following:

> India and Nigeria are not democracy that share internal conflicts between diverse ethnics and religion groups. Two countries faced same path of

colonialism and created parliamentary democracy. *[I'm not that familiar with this part of history, so maybe I'm missing something, but . . . are you saying that colonialism created parliamentary democracy? You might want to explain how colonialism brought this form of government about. Just a thought.]* At a time of independence, they were not ready to control over the country, since then they faced *[it's interesting to read about the link between present-day problems and past history—could you say more about this?]* several difficulties to maintain the democracy. Their position as democracy are not stable, moreover, the possibility to fail is likely today.

What is interesting about this version is that both comments make the same point, and it is the connection the writer seems to be trying to make between the colonialism of the past and the parliamentary democracies of the present. This tells the writer that a key idea is in play in this paragraph and needs attention. Imagine, then, this paragraph once more, and this time with just one comment at the end.

India and Nigeria are not democracy that share internal conflicts between diverse ethnics and religion groups. Two countries faced the same path of colonialism and created parliamentary democracy. At a time of independence, they were not ready to control over the country, since then they faced several difficulties to maintain the democracy. Their position as democracy are not stable today, moreover, the possibility to fail is likely. *[It sounds like you are trying to make an important point about the link between present-day problems and past history. If so, I think you should include more facts and examples about the role of the past in shaping the form of government these two countries have today because this point needs more support.]*

With this comment, the tutor shows that she recognizes the writer is attempting to make a point and tries to confirm what it is. But the comment does something else, too, and that is to help the writer see that communicating his idea is the most important thing to attend to in this paragraph. To reach this point, however, the tutor has to ignore the many other opportunities for comments that she sees and concentrate on helping the writer get his main idea across. Learning to respond in this way means that tutors may need to read students' papers differently than they are accustomed to. This is but one of the lessons we learned from our online tutoring experience. I would like to conclude this chapter with a few others, and some advice for those who may be embarking on online tutoring.

Lessons Learned from the Online Experience

The following are based on our experiences tutoring online for both ESL and native speaking writers.

1. Writing lots of feedback items in online responses is ineffective. We found that tutors who responded in this way wrote more than most writers

actually followed through on when making revisions. Writers in our follow-up interviews explained that they appreciated the detailed feedback tutors provided but often addressed only a handful of the many points their tutors worked so laboriously to make. When asked why he made only a couple of changes and did not address the rest, for example, one writer acknowledged he should have, but said just didn't get around to it before the paper was due.

The advice to tutors working online, then, is to avoid making lots of comments on a paper. They are time-consuming to write, difficult to prioritize, and easy to ignore. While writers may appreciate the effort a tutor makes to write lots of comments, they are not necessarily prepared to read or think about following through on all of them. Writers get better little by little, and frequent tutorial sessions that focus on small changes are better than fewer sessions that focus on many at once.

2. Writers who receive detailed feedback, with suggestions ranging from minor editing to global revision, often make the editing changes but not the global revisions. In follow-up interviews, some students did not see a distinction between a suggestion to change a word or phrase and a suggestion to develop an idea or revise a thesis statement. This is consistent with the findings of Nancy Sommers, who wrote, "On every occasion when I asked students why they hadn't made any more changes, they essentially replied, 'I knew something larger was wrong, but I didn't think it would help to move words around.'" [8]

Although it may sometimes seem as though writers are interested only in word- or phrase-level revisions because these are the easiest to make, beginning writers may in fact be focused on this level because they see it as the *only* level, as Sommers observed. Moreover, feedback that mixes comments directed at occasional surface errors with comments about larger rhetorical matters (such as organization, focus, and the development of ideas) may lead writers to assume they can mitigate rhetorical problems by correcting surface problems or by simply moving words around. But if they cannot see how moving words around makes any difference, then they may assume the rhetorical problem cannot be fixed, or at least not by them.

The advice to tutors, then, is to keep comments about rhetorical matters distinct from other comments. Unless a word, phrase, or sentence is clearly preventing the writer from conveying what seems to be a key point, let it go and focus on those places where key points are getting lost. In addition, show the writer how changing a few words around begins to improve the text, and then identify the rest of the confusing text that needs to be worked on. If the paper contains lots of places where key points are unclear, then pick one or two and focus on them, leaving the rest alone. If you believe it is necessary to comment about a word or phrase when no key point is at stake, then tell the author what the relative priority of this comment is. Carol Severino (Chapter 5) adds this important qualification:

> The assignment, focus, argument, development, and organization are usually more important than expression unless some language clarifications and corrections are needed simply in order to understand whether the student has followed the assignment and to understand her points. In the case of language completely obscuring argument, the level of language would be considered a higher order and global concern. Otherwise, there is no point in working carefully and slowly to reformulate language that should not or probably will not appear in the next draft because the student needs to refocus or revise her entire argument.

3.   Writers assess their tutors' trustworthiness. We tend to take for granted that students value the feedback they receive from tutors, and most do. At the same time, they view tutorial feedback with a consumer's eye, mindful that the quality of advice they receive depends on their tutor's knowledge and skills. Our follow-up interviews indicated that tutors who acknowledge unfamiliarity with a topic can sow seeds of doubts in some writers' minds. Tutors who indicate frankly that they don't know much about the topic, as the tutor did in the response ("I'm not familiar with this history, so maybe I'm missing something . . . ") may cause some writers to then doubt the value of the tutor's comments on other aspects of their writing and become hesitant to make the suggested revisions. Writers sometimes read tentativeness as wishy-washy, as when tutors wrote statements like, "You might want to think about changing. . . . " Or, "I wonder if some readers might think this means. . . . " Since the tutor seemed so unsure about the comment, they reasoned, they would leave that part of the paper alone.[9]

Advice: Honesty is essential, and tutors should disclose their limitations to the writer when they feel it is necessary. At the same time, when tutors do have something constructive to offer the writer, they should say it plainly and confidently, and explain why. As for the tentativeness or hesitation writers hear in phrases like "you might want to think about . . . " or "I wonder if . . . ," it is worth remembering that phrases a tutor uses to indicate nondirectiveness, others may interpret as wishy-washy.

4.   Finally, writers often don't make changes because they do not hear a consistent and repeated message. For example, in one paper, following the greeting, a tutor identified a paragraph near the end that didn't seem to fit with the overall flow of ideas in the paper. When asked in the follow-up interview why he had decided not to make any changes to that paragraph before he handed it in, the student replied that his instructor had said this was a particularly good paragraph in a previous draft of the paper, and so he did not want to change it. In this writer's mind, a good paragraph is a good paragraph, and since the tutor's advice seemed to him to conflict with his instructor's, he followed the instructor's. At other times, we found

that writers perceived inconsistencies within their tutor's message. At the beginning of one paper, the tutor had written the following:

> I really enjoyed reading your paper, Jo. You picked an interesting topic to write about. As you can see, I just made a few comments for you. I hope they make sense. These changes shouldn't be too hard to make, so don't cancel your plans for the weekend ☺. Good luck with this assignment!

When Jo read the tutor's comments, however, she saw that they involved making global revisions that would indeed take time. But since the tutor said they shouldn't be too hard to make, Jo told us in the follow-up interview, she decided to make a few minor editing changes and that's all. In other words, the writer responded more to the tutor's attempt to be reassuring and comforting than to the real need for revisions the tutor had identified.

The best advice: make suggestions clear to the writer and don't try to sugarcoat them. More important, deliver a consistent message and reinforce it throughout the paper so that the writer can see how important it is.

In the end, tutors learned to improve their responses to ESL and all papers submitted online in much the same we all learn to write, by drafting their responses, seeking feedback, and improving them as they went along. It is a process that can improve all tutoring, face-to-face or online.

Notes

1. We began online tutoring in January 1999, thanks to the assistance of Jennifer Ritter, Dennis Ausel, and a grant from the Indiana University of Pennsylvania Faculty Professional Development Council. After grant funding expired in 2000, we continued to conduct online tutoring on an occasional basis with one or two classes each year.

2. While some students provided assignment details and a clear sense of direction for tutors to work with, most did not. They tended to write requests like, "Please look over my paper. Any help you can give me with grammar or whatever you see would be appreciated" or "I need help with organizing my thoughts, and punctuation."

3. For a good discussion of protocols for inserting comments into a paper, see Cooper, Bui, and Riker (2000) and Monroe (1998).

4. The tutor's comments in this paragraph reflect a composite of responses we developed, after studying many students' papers and tutors' responses, for training.

5. Wingate (2000).

6. See Ritter (2000).

7. The question of how to go about helping ESL writers to correct grammar is discussed in Leki (1992), chap. 10.

8. Sommers (1980).

9. The mixed messages that nondirective feedback can create are confirmed by Ferris and Hedgcock, 144–45.

Works Cited

Cooper, George, Kara Bui, and Linda Riker. 2000. "Protocols and Process in Online Tutoring." In *A Tutor's Guide: Helping Writers One to One*, edited by B. Rafoth, 91–101. Portsmouth, NH: Boynton/Cook.

Ferris, Dana, and John S. Hedgcock. 1998. *Teaching ESL Composition*. Mahwah, NJ: Lawrence Erlbaum.

Leki, Ilona. 1992. *Understanding ESL Writers*. Portsmouth, NH: Boynton/Cook.

Monroe, Barbara. 1998. "The Look and Feel of the OWL Conference." In *Wiring the Center*, edited by E. Hobson, 3–24. Logan, UT: Utah State University Press.

Ritter, Jennifer. 2000. "Recent Developments in Assisting ESL Writers." In *A Tutor's Guide: Helping Writers One to One*, edited by B. Rafoth, 102–10. Portsmouth, NH: Boynton/Cook.

Sommers, Nancy. 1980. "Revision Strategies of Student Writers and Experienced Adult Writers." *College Composition and Communication* 31: 378–88.

Wingate, Molly. 2000. "What Line? I Didn't See Any Line." In *A Tutor's Guide: Helping Writers One to One*, edited by B. Rafoth, 9–16. Portsmouth, NH: Boynton/Cook.

10

Raising Questions About Plagiarism

Kurt Bouman

Maybe it's a word that stands out, or a sentence that sounds as though a skilled native speaker of English could have written it. Maybe it's a phrase that's familiar to you from another student's writing, or from a source you have read. Perhaps it's just an inkling that something about the writing is incongruous, that one or two parts don't seem consistent with the rest of the paper, or with the ESL writer next to you. What happens now? Do you set aside your suspicions and continue with the tutoring session, assuming that the writer may simply be working with sources in ways different than you expect? How do you respond if it's an entire paper that you have seen before, during another consultation with a different student? Maybe you feel a flush of embarrassment, confusion, or indignation; perhaps you look for a reason to step over to a fellow tutor, or to your director, for a quick consultation of your own: "I'm not sure what to do; I don't think this student wrote these words!" Or do you question the writer directly, asking, "Where did you get these words? They don't quite seem to match your writing. Are they your own?"

Plagiarism is a hot topic; in the past few years, high-profile writers such as Doris Kearns Goodwin and Stephen Ambrose have been accused of plagiarism, and, in one of the most scandalous cases of falsified writing, plagiarism forced journalist Jayson Blair to resign from his position at the *New York Times*. Most plagiarism, however, doesn't make the national news. In fact, few cases are ever made public at all. Yet this doesn't mean they're not important, for even plagiarism in college can leave a student facing severe penalties—penalties that, for some foreign students, may even jeopardize their ability to continue their studies.

Questions about plagiarism can leave students hurt, confused, alienated, or offended, even when they have cited all of their sources correctly and completely. These feelings of social and psychological distress may be especially acute for ESL writers, who often work very hard to produce the kinds of writing that their professors expect. Fortunately, as a peer writing tutor, you are in a good position to help ESL students learn more about your institution's values and conventions regarding using sources in writing, and to help them practice the particular rhetorical skills—paraphrasing, summarizing, and quoting—that accompany these values. In the context of a one-on-one writing consultation and with appropriate training, you can feel comfortable raising the issue of plagiarism and discussing the conventions, beliefs, and values that make some people react to it so strongly.

Understanding Plagiarism

Before we go further into a discussion of plagiarism, it's important to think about what plagiarism is: plagiarism is commonly defined as presenting the words or ideas of another person as though they are the writer's own. While this definition may seem straightforward, it raises important questions about cultural and academic values and textual practices:

- What does it mean to present words or ideas as though they are one's own?
- How can a person own things like words or ideas?
- How many words can one safely copy from a source?
- Why do some people make such a big deal about plagiarism? What is it that makes a writing teacher as celebrated as Peter Elbow describe plagiarism as "the worst academic sin of all"?[1]

To begin with, the word *plagiarism* does not have one clear-cut meaning; instead, people use it to describe a range of practices:

- using ideas from a source without acknowledging the source
- copying specific words or phrases from a source without using quotation marks
- doing a word-for-word substitution in an attempt to paraphrase a source, but keeping the source's basic ideas and sentence structure intact[2]
- "patchwriting," or building a paper by patching together sections of text from one or more sources[3]
- submitting a paper downloaded off the Internet

Plagiarism and Culture

As you tutor, you'll encounter writers with a wide range of skills and experiences in working with source texts. Some writers will be able to move fluently and clearly between their own ideas and those of their sources, skillfully weaving these different voices together with a combination of summary, paraphrasing, and quoting. Experienced writers know that their college audiences expect this, and they have often spent years practicing the conventions of citation, making sure they get it right. Yet many of the writers you'll work with, both native and nonnative English speakers, will get it wrong. Most of them, too, will try hard to avoid plagiarism; they'll be sure to include their sources in a bibliography, and, when they bring in ideas from sources, they'll often—but not always—change a few words. But they won't always get it right, and some of them, particularly the ESL writers you work with, may find plagiarism a particularly confounding concept.

In the United States and in many English-language schools throughout the world, ideas about plagiarism (and plagiarism policies) are driven by a particular understanding about what it means to write. In many Western contexts, for instance, we place a strong value on individuality and independence, and we encourage writers to develop and use their "authentic voice," a way of writing that is uniquely their own. "[V]oice," writes Peter Elbow, "is an *ideal* metaphor for individualism. Every person's voice is literally, physically unique — perhaps more reliably than fingerprints"[4]—and most Western readers expect writers to express themselves in their own voices, rather than through the voices of others. So, when one considers *why* voice might matter so much in writing, one reason for our attitudes toward plagiarism might become clearer: that plagiarism misappropriates voice—a unique and individual characteristic of a writer—and that it thereby undermines an important goal of writing.

While individuality is an important value in Western education, so, too, is originality, and many teachers expect writers to say things that are original, not simply to parrot ideas and words they've found elsewhere.[5] Western audiences expect writers to create new meaning through their use of sources, to contribute their own ideas to the discussion. Generally, U.S. students "are rewarded for their own creativity and fresh voice," Sarah Graff writes.[6] Because of this reward, it's important to make sure that we appropriately acknowledge the source of the ideas and words we use. We want to make sure we give credit where credit is due, and we want to avoid taking credit for work other people have done.

While individuality and originality are important to many Western audiences, other societies hold different beliefs about the purposes of writing— beliefs that may appear quite foreign to Westerners. According to Glenn Deckert, "The Western tradition typically honors a person's divergent thinking through that individual's arbitration and participation in ongoing academic exchange. Other traditions, as in China, emphasize close allegiance to a few acknowledged authorities with resulting convergence of perspective and greater social harmony."[7] Such cultures generally value collectivity over individuality, a perspective that holds that it is better to work for the common good rather than for individual gain.

These different cultural values lead to different writing practices. For example, Guanjun Cai writes that in China, where knowledge is based on "collective wisdom and social norms"[8] rather than in the mind of any particular individual person, writers are expected to suppress their individuality rather than celebrate it. There, "Confucianism still promotes the use of proverbs to carry on age old messages about morality and universal truths. In Korea, students are graded highly by their teachers if they imitate classic writers."[9] Western students, by contrast, are expected to develop their own ideas, and to express them in their own ways.

When we ask students from collectivist cultures to write with originality and individuality, we ask them to work with a set of beliefs about writing that may be quite different than what they are used to. Just like all writers, ESL students rely on what they have been taught about writing; yet that knowledge sometimes contradicts the expectations of a Western audience. For instance, Glenn Deckert asserts that many Chinese students plagiarize unintentionally by repeating source material verbatim: "They are the proverbial rote memorizers or recyclers," he writes. "In the school setting, they are unaccustomed to deriving and expressing their own insight into academic issues."[10] Sometimes, then, particular ways of writing that violate basic Western plagiarism standards may be seen as correct and appropriate by other (non-Western) audiences.[11] As one Chinese student reports:

> I consider it important to memorize sentences to write better. . . . If the English teacher required me to write a long English essay . . . I would turn to famous sayings and sentences derived from famous writers and essays on the same topic. I would imitate what other people say and use their sentences in my essays. I would at most change a single word but I would not change the main frame or structure. . . . If my English teacher required me to write long English essays, I would use famous sayings, proverbs, and quotable phrases quite often, just as I use them very often in writing Chinese essays, for I consider they are essential in writing Chinese and English essays.[12]

Cross-cultural differences, however, do not account for all of the plagiarism we sometimes see in writing center tutorials. ESL students give other reasons for plagiarizing; one reason is the amount of time required to complete assignments in a second language:

- Diana, a native Cantonese speaker originally from Macau, was struggling with a significant workload. She began to copy parts of her papers, noting "her need to write the assignments more 'efficiently.' For Diana, . . . copying meant saving time."[13]

Other students describe plagiarizing assignments because they feel as though their instructors don't care about the writing or about their students:

- A student from Kyrgyzstan states, "[P]rofessors required us to show that we were familiar with the subject and they were happy . . . even if we showed that we went to the library. . . . [T]hey didn't care whether we just copied all these texts or wrote it by ourselves."[14]
- A Bulgarian graduate student acknowledges copying parts of an assignment from the Internet because his instructor "didn't care about you [and] didn't do her job. . . . [S]he hasn't put efforts, I'm not putting efforts either."[15]

In these two cases, the students' plagiarism might be described as cheating; after all, they copied text deliberately, fully aware that they were not writing the assignment on their own. However, Alastair Pennycook offers another interpretation for such plagiarism: given that the students were attending universities in post-Communist countries, and given that they were intentionally violating the conventions and expectations of their universities, their plagiarism might be understood as "a justifiably cynical form of resistance"[16] in which the student writers were acting to undermine the dominating effect of the educational system.

The Challenge of Paraphrasing Properly

The complexity of academic English presents a formidable challenge for many ESL writers (as it does for many native English-speaking students as well). Even professional scholars sometimes plagiarize as they struggle with writing in English; a Taiwanese computer scientist states:

> After working hard in research, locally trained researchers with poor English writing skill still need to struggle very hard for translating their research findings into English [so that they can be published in Western academic journals]. It is even more disappointing when their papers are rejected simply because of writing problems. As a result, imitating the "sentence structures" from well-written papers seems a good way to escape from the writing problems.[17]

"If faculty [even] have difficulty comprehending and manipulating the languages of the various academic cultures," Rebecca Moore Howard writes about native speakers, "how much more difficult a task do undergraduate students face as they are presented with a bewildering array of discourse, none of which resonates with the languages of their homes and secondary schools?"[18] Think about some of the difficult texts you have been asked to read in college, and remember some of the ways you have struggled with academic discourse; now, imagine how much more difficult these tasks would be if you were reading and writing in a second (or third) language.

When students write in academic settings, David Bartholomae points out, they must "learn to speak our language, to speak as we do."[19] For some ESL writers, changing a few words of a source text, but keeping intact the structure and tone of the original, represents a starting point, an entryway into a new language community. Yet most plagiarism policies expect students to paraphrase well and appropriately—that is, to recast a source text in their own voice, using their own words. However, paraphrasing is one of the most complex writing skills there is,[20] because, as Mary M. Dossin says, it requires that a writer "both master his sources and break his connection to their language and structure."[21] To paraphrase well and correctly, writers must employ a number of high-level language skills:

- They need to understand the meaning of all of the words and ideas in a source text.

- They need to accurately discern the author's tone and stance in the writing.
- They need to come up with lexical and syntactic equivalents of the source text—alternative words and sentence structures—so that they can express the source's meaning in "original" language.

When ESL writers make a too-close paraphrase, or even when they patch in source text directly, their "plagiarism" may well represent the beginning of participation in a new academic culture, rather than an attempt to subvert that culture's expectations about originality and authorship. When one's vocabulary is limited, or when a writer's familiarity with the syntax of a language is insufficient to allow her to explore multiple versions of a sentence, then, according to Howard, the writer may "have no choice but to patch monologically from the text."[22] When this happens, we should welcome the writer's attempt to move into a new language, and we should do all we can to help the writer navigate the difficult and unfamiliar terrain of academic writing in English.

Suggestions for Tutoring ESL Writers

Be Direct and Explicit When Discussing Problems with Using Sources

Plagiarism can be a sensitive topic, and many of us might not feel comfortable raising questions about plagiarism. We don't want to risk offending students, particularly those who have worked diligently on their assignments. We should keep in mind, however, that plagiarism is not a "shameful topic,"[23] and that it is both appropriate and important for a tutor to discuss using sources correctly with a writer when there are any questions about whether the writer has plagiarized, intentionally or not. Discussing your questions directly will ensure that the writer knows that you have some concerns about his use of sources, and it will let the two of you begin to work together to help him better understand his audience's expectations.

To open a conversation about suspected plagiarism, you might simply ask the writer, "Did you consult any sources as you wrote this paper?" If she answers "yes," you might follow up by asking her to indicate in her paper any words, phrases, or ideas she found in her sources. If she replies, "No," you can show her why you asked the question, pointing out which parts of her paper caught your eye, and helping her find ways to make those parts fit more smoothly. During this conversation, remember to maintain a supportive, encouraging, nonjudgmental role. You might do this most easily by keeping in mind that using sources, like any other aspect of writing, represents a developmental continuum, and that some writers will be better at it than others.

Several resources can facilitate your conversations about plagiarism and sources. First, you might refer to your school's plagiarism policy. (This can usually be found in the student handbook.) Discussing the specific wording the policy uses to describe plagiarism can make the institution's expectations clearer to ESL students who may not fully understand the language of the policy on their own. You might also consult one or two composition handbooks; reviewing various descriptions of plagiarism and documentation will offer alternative explanations, as well as a variety of examples to illustrate correct and incorrect use of sources. Finally, you might consider developing an archive of sample papers for the writing center—papers from different disciplines, written and documented according to different styles (MLA, APA, Chicago, etc.). This "corpus" will allow tutors and writers to analyze real writing samples to discover different ways to integrate source information into a paper.[24]

Ask the ESL Writer About His Understanding of Plagiarism, and About How He Is Accustomed to Writing with Sources

One effective way to raise the topic of plagiarism in a tutoring session is to invite the writer to talk about some of the writing conventions he learned in his home culture.[25] To facilitate this conversation, consider asking some of the following questions about academic writing in terms of the student's home culture. The writer's responses to these questions will provide points of comparison through which you can discuss cultural differences about using sources.

- What has the writer been taught about how writers should use sources in their academic writing?

- Are writers expected to consult sources as they write, or are they expected to develop their papers based primarily on their own ideas?

- If writers use sources, do they mainly summarize the sources' arguments, or should they use the information to develop their own ideas in their papers?

- Are writers expected to use direct quotes? If so, must they use quotation marks?

- How do writers acknowledge their sources? Do they create footnotes or a "works cited" page?

- Is it ever appropriate for a writer to copy words or ideas directly from a source without citing the source?

- Does the writer's native language have a word for *plagiarism*? If so, what does it mean? What was the writer taught about U.S. academic conventions for using the words or ideas of others?

During a Consultation, Look at a Writer's Sources Side-by-Side with Her Papers

One of the best ways to help a writer learn to use sources effectively and appropriately is to look at the writer's sources alongside her text. Begin by asking the writer to indicate where in her paper she used words or ideas from sources; for instance, she might underline all of the source words in her paper. Colored highlighters work well, too, especially if you want to distinguish between direct quotes and paraphrases or summaries. If computers are available, you might suggest the writer indicate use of sources with a different font. Whatever your method, the point is the same: to draw the writer's attention to the traces of her source texts in her own paper. Even first-language writers sometimes find it difficult to summarize or paraphrase a source text without drawing too heavily on the source's original language or sentence structure; looking at source and paper side-by-side will allow immediate, accurate comparisons, and will make any too-close paraphrases (and missing citations) readily apparent.

In addition to making it easier for the writer to pick up inadvertent plagiarism, highlighting source text will help you focus on the writer's use of her sources, and will let you focus on the following questions:

- Does the writer do a good job of weaving the source information into his paper?
- Does she vary the way she uses sources, drawing on summary, paraphrasing, and direct quotation?
- Does he choose appropriate times to use direct quotes in his paper, or does he overuse them, failing to make an original argument in his paper?

With the writer's sources in front of you, the two of you can best ensure that her paper uses source material accurately and correctly, in ways that are both rhetorically effective and academically appropriate.

Responding to Plagiarism

Most students who plagiarize do so inadvertently: they don't intend to break any rules, but their language skills or knowledge of citation conventions may not allow them to work with sources in ways appropriate to the context they're writing in. Yet some students, native and nonnative English speakers alike, knowingly disregard citation conventions, or sometimes deliberately pass off someone else's writing as their own. This kind of plagiarism—what Rebecca Moore Howard suggests we call "fraud"[26]—puts writing tutors in a difficult position. The best way you can prepare for such a situation is to consider your options ahead of time. With your writing center director, and with fellow tutors, discuss how you might respond to the following scenarios:

- An ESL student brings in a paper for a second consultation with you. As you read the paper, you notice that the writing is much clearer and more complex than it was in a previous draft. When you mention this to the student, she tells you that she asked her roommate, an English major, to edit the paper for her and to make any needed changes to her wording and sentence structure.

- As you read over a student's paper, you notice that several paragraphs seem to be substantially different from the others. As you look more closely at these paragraphs, you notice that they are printed in a slightly different font. When you ask the student about this, he says that he was having trouble coming up with ideas for the paper, so he copied a few paragraphs from a website.

- At the beginning of your tutoring session, you ask your tutee to tell you a little bit about her paper. She isn't able to describe her topic very clearly, and she can't recall any of the specific details or examples she used. When you ask her about certain words she used in the paper, she doesn't seem to know what they mean.

As you have these conversations in your writing center, ask your director if there are any established procedures or guidelines you should follow if you suspect that a writer has plagiarized. In particular, discuss whether (and, if so, how) you should document your conversation with the writer. Because some instructors are suspicious of writing center assistance (thinking that writing centers help students plagiarize), and because some colleges have honor codes that require students to report suspected plagiarism, it may be helpful to keep clear, detailed, and confidential notes about any consultation during which you suspect plagiarism.

If you suspect a student of intentional plagiarism, the most appropriate response might be to handle it in the same way you would handle inadvertent plagiarism: offer to help the student understand your school's plagiarism policy, and offer to work with the student on appropriate ways to use source texts. Since tutors work with writers in the drafting and revising stages of writing— generally before work has been submitted for final evaluation—there may still be time for the writer to complete the assignment on his own, following the rules of documentation as well as those of academic integrity.

What a challenge writers face when they move into a new academic culture: they must adapt to a new language, new ways of developing papers, and new ways of relating to the texts they read. As we work with ESL writers, we need to keep in mind that we're asking them to work in an environment that may be quite different than the one they're accustomed to, and we need to remember that the rules of that culture, and its conventions for using sources, may appear quite foreign. In their book *Tutoring Writing*, Donald McAndrew and Thomas Reigstad point out that all cultures have rhetorical preferences, "all of which are equally good," and that our preferences are neither better nor worse than those of any other culture.[27] As insiders to the academic community, writing tutors are in an ideal position to serve as "cultural/rhetorical informants,"[28] helping students understand the citation and documentation conventions of the academy. In our tutorials, then, we would do well to build on the higher-order concerns and lower-order concerns that we're most familiar with; we should also help students gain a better understanding of our institutions' expectations regarding the use of sources in writing.

Discussing and practicing citation conventions can help all writers avoid plagiarism, regardless of their language backgrounds. It can also help ESL writers develop the kind of original, independent voice that many of their English-language instructors expect them to use. It will result in better writing, too—not just more "correct" writing, but also writing that uses sources in more complex and rhetorically effective ways.

Notes

1. Elbow, 330.
2. Howard (2000), 82.
3. Howard (1992), 233.
4. Elbow, 334–35.
5. Spigelman, 4.
6. Graff (2002).
7. Deckert, 132. Here, Deckert is paraphrasing L. K. Hsu, *Americans and Chinese* (Honolulu: University Press of Hawaii, 1981).
8. Cai, 281.
9. Graff (2002).
10. Deckert, 133.
11. Cai, 280.
12. Ho, p. 234, cited in Ramanathan and Atkinson, 54–55. Here, Ramanathan and Atkinson are quoting from I. Ho, *Relationships Between Motivation/Attitude, Effort, English Proficiency, and Socio-Cultural Educational Factors and Taiwan Technological University/Institute Students' English Learning Strategy Use* (Auburn University, unpublished dissertation, 1998).
13. Currie, 9.
14. Minett (2002).
15. Minett (2002).
16. Pennycook, 282.
17. Myers, 14.
18. Howard (1992), 233.
19. Bartholomae, 134.
20. Myers, 9.
21. Dossin, 129.
22. Howard (1992), 240.
23. Hyland, 380.
24. Thompson and Tribble (2001).
25. Crowley, 3.
26. Howard (2002), 488.

27. McAndrew and Reigstad, 6. Here, McAndrew and Reigstad are paraphrasing Harris and Silva, "Tutoring ESL Students: Issues and Options," *College Composition and Communication* 44 (1993): 525–37.

28. Powers, 42.

Works Cited

Bartholomae, David. 1985. "Inventing the University." In *When a Writer Can't Write*, edited by Mike Rose, 134–65. New York: Guilford Press.

Cai, Guanjun. 1999. "Texts in Contexts: Understanding Chinese Students' English Compositions." In *Evaluating Writing: The Role of Teachers' Knowledge about Text, Learning, and Culture*, edited by Charles Cooper and Lee Odell, 279–97. Urbana, IL: NCTE.

Crowley, Catherine. 2001. "'Are We on the Same Page?' ESL Student Perceptions of the Writing Center." *Writing Lab Newsletter* 25 (9): 1–5.

Currie, Pat. 1998. "Staying Out of Trouble: Apparent Plagiarism and Academic Survival." *Journal of Second Language Writing* 7 (1): 1–18.

Deckert, Glenn D. 1993. "Perspectives on Plagiarism from ESL Students in Hong Kong." *Journal of Second Language Writing* 2 (2): 131–48.

Dossin, Mary Mortimore. 2000. "Using Others' Words: Quoting, Summarizing, and Documenting Sources." In *A Tutor's Guide: Helping Writers One to One*, edited by Ben Rafoth, 127–34. Portsmouth, NH: Boynton/Cook.

Elbow, Peter. 1999. "Individualism and the Teaching of Writing: Response to Vai Ramanathan and Dwight Atkinson." *Journal of Second Language Writing* 8 (3): 327–38.

Graff, Sarah. 2002. E-mail post reprinted in "*TESL-EJ* Forum: Perspectives on Plagiarism in the ESL/EFL Classroom," edited by Karen Stanley. *TESL-EJ* 6 (3): 5. www-writing.berkeley.edu/TESL-EJ.

Howard, Rebecca Moore. 1992. "A Plagiarism Pentimento." *Journal of Teaching Writing* 11 (2): 233–45.

———. 2000. "The Ethics of Plagiarism." In *The Ethics of Writing Instruction: Issues in Theory and Practice*, edited by Michael E. Pemberton, 79–90. Stamford, CT: Ablex.

———. 2002. "Sexuality, Textuality: The Cultural Work of Plagiarism." *College English* 62 (4): 473–91.

Hyland, Fiona. 2001. "Dealing with Plagiarism when Giving Feedback." *ELT Journal* 55 (4): 375–81.

McAndrew, Donald A., and Thomas J. Reigstad. 2001. *Tutoring Writing: A Practical Guide for Conferences*. Portsmouth, NH: Boynton/Cook.

Minett, Amy. 2002. Plagiarism and Pedagogy: Central European Perspectives and Practice. Paper presented at European Association for the Teaching of Academic Writing Conference, June 17–20, Groningen, The Netherlands.

Myers, Sharon. 1998. "Questioning Author(ity): ESL/EFL, Science, and Teaching About Plagiarism." *TESL-EJ* 3 (2). www-writing.berkeley.edu/TESL-EJ.

Pennycook, Alastair. 1994. "The Complex Contexts of Plagiarism: A Reply to Deckert." *Journal of Second Language Writing* 3 (3): 277–84.

Powers, Judith K. 1993. "Rethinking Writing Center Conferencing Strategies for the ESL Writer." *The Writing Center Journal* 13 (2): 39–47.

Ramanathan, Vai, and Dwight Atkinson. 1999. "Individualism, Academic Writing, and ESL Writers." *Journal of Second Language Writing* 8 (1): 45–75.

Spigelman, Candace. 2000. *Across Property Lines: Textual Ownership in Writing Groups.* Carbondale, IL: Southern Illinois University Press.

Thompson, Paul, and Chris Tribble. 2001. "Looking at Citations: Using Corpora in English for Academic Purposes." *Language Learning & Technology* 5 (3): 91–105.

11

Is This My Job?

Paula Gillespie

This is a question we ask often in writing center work, but international students are by no means the only ones who make us wonder about the boundaries of our tutoring jobs. Consider the writer from a town five miles from campus, who schedules himself for five sessions with you in a week. Is that your job? Consider the writer who comes up to you in the coffee shop and hands you her paper, wants you to answer just a few questions. . . . But ESL writers, either because of institutional pressures to produce perfect writing or because of cultural misunderstandings, may also raise this vexing question for you.

I'll admit it: I can relate to the ESL writer, and perhaps you can, too. When I'm traveling in a foreign country, I find myself asking a lot of questions, questions that take up the precious time of the person I'm asking, and I'll also admit it: sometimes I don't understand the explanations. I nod and say "Ja" or "Oui"; even if I don't know, I agree. I need a lot of help abroad, even if I know the language. I ask for things in Germany I'd never dream of asking for at home. "Is this the right change?" "What is this word on the train schedule?" "Would you help me find. . . ?"

I remember an incident that helps me to understand how naïve and vulnerable even sophisticated international students can feel when they use an unfamiliar language: I was in the Sudtirol area of Italy and had been speaking German for a few weeks, managing to make myself (and my friends) understood pretty well by the locals. I'd learned a lot of essential new vocabulary words and had made liberal use of my German-English pocket dictionary. One evening two German couples who had been staying at my *pensione* were saying goodbye; they had become good friends and were taking pictures of one another. I asked them, in German, if they'd like me to take a group picture of all four of them. Ja! They accepted my offer happily, and handed me two cameras. *"Kopfen zusammen!"* I said, cheerfully. "Heads together," I thought. But they burst spontaneously into gales of laughter, and I knew something was wrong, but I had no clue what it was. I took the pictures (I didn't need to ask them to smile!) and headed back to my room. *Zusammen.* I knew that word. "Together." Yep. But *Kopf*? Head? I knew that word, too. But when I looked it up in my dictionary, there was the source of their high hilarity. The plural was not the regular *Kopfen,* but *Koepfe,* a word with a very different sound in German. I had said the equivalent of "foots together." The fact that they knew I was an English professor surely added to their merriment: I'd spoken German baby talk!

This incident helped me understand that international students are concerned with more than getting good grades when they ask us to help them with correctness: they don't want to look silly or be laughable in their writing. I thought the situation in the Sudtirol was pretty funny, too, once I got the joke, but in an academic setting where I was trying to establish myself as a serious scholar, the stakes would have been much higher, and I probably wouldn't be looking back and laughing now.

So when international writers come to the writing center and ask for services we don't usually offer, and sometimes make us ask: "Is this my job?" I like to imagine myself in their situation. On first thought, we might assume that the answers could be determined pretty simply by your center's policy: do you proofread or offer error analysis? How long can a session run? Is there a limit to the number of sessions writers are allowed in a given time? In these cases the answer is simple. Or is it?

There *is* one instance when the answer is relatively simple: Is the requested service someone else's job? Suppose a writer has finished a draft and wants to make ongoing appointments to hold conversations, with the goal of improving her spoken fluency and correcting her pronunciation. She's not asking to work on writing, or at least not now: she wants to work on her speech. On many campuses, an office of international programs offers that service. On other campuses, foreign language departments do. The people involved set up conversation groups between international students who want to improve their English and native speakers who want to improve their Italian or Greek conversational ability. The pairs or groups take turns practicing and improving. It sounds like fun. Sometimes a campus will have a speech therapy program or clinic that will offer sessions to help international speakers with pronouncing the sounds of English that they find difficult. This is different from wanting to improve fluency in conversation, and it takes a different kind of expertise. If these services are offered (and a search of your school's website might give you an answer to this question in advance, before this question comes up), then it seems simple to refer writers to these places. But what if they are not offered? Perhaps your director would be flexible about allowing these sessions. It would surely depend on how busy your center is, on the demand for writing help. But it wouldn't hurt to ask. You'd learn a lot, if you took such a project on, just as you do from tutoring writing. You could ask interesting questions about a culture you might want to learn about and have the fun of listening to an expert give first-person accounts of home.

But what about those requests that are a bit more complicated? The following are some examples.

The first is from Stephanie, who is fluent in Italian:

> With one student I really remember asking myself, "Is *this* my job?" Because her language skills were so basic, my main task became translating concepts from Italian to English. She wrote her ideas in English, verbatim, as they would translate from Italian. The idiosyncrasies of both languages do not allow for this method, so her sentences rarely made sense. This student's professors would require her to come to the writing center. She would bring in three- to four-page essays that we could not read through—for she had no idea where she was making mistakes, no matter who read the paper. We would stop on almost every line and I would ask her to verbalize her meaning—[she] often [spoke] half in Italian and half in English. Then I would translate the concept for her, which she would write down. The problem, in my mind, was that the majority of the workload was placed on me, the tutor, in our sessions—I felt I was writing a portion of her papers. Nor was I sure of how much learning . . . was happening for her since she was only hearing the concepts once—not regularly practicing the language. I was happy to help her, but I'm not sure the dilemma was ever resolved.

Stephanie is right that she is supplying phrases for this writer, and she's right that it's a frustrating situation, but I wonder if she's right that no learning was going on. It seems that this writer does not have a grasp of the basic structure of the English sentence; she has limited resources for mastering English syntax, and she may have no other resources for learning. I believe that Stephanie's approach might have been moving this writer forward; exercises or memorization, ways she might have originally learned English, would not be as beneficial to her as it would be to work on her own writing, applying some rules Stephanie could help her with. The writer's progress will undoubtedly be slow compared to that of some others, and she will need some teaching rather than minimalist tutoring, but perhaps over time she will improve, feel more comfortable, and begin to think in English structures. Sometimes we have the good fortune to work with writers like this over a long period, and the improvement can be dramatic, though not necessarily fast. Does this writer have native speakers she can talk to, or is she living only with speakers of Italian? We can suggest that the writer might find a conversation partner, that she should watch television and read simple things for fun. Is working with her writing Stephanie's job? It seems to be, even though it is very difficult to find the right balance of help to offer.

Jerry, an undergraduate peer tutor, has a complex problem that may sound familiar:

> About 90 percent of the tutoring sessions I've had this year involved ESL students. Although all of them were very friendly and grateful for any help they

could get, I was always intimidated because their needs often went beyond those of students more familiar with the language.

Many of them came to me with extensive master's theses on subjects I could never comprehend, but thankfully the only real input they wanted concerned grammar issues. Given that the material was so complex, this was often the only help I could give in the first place. The problem was that it was often mentally draining to devote hours on end to grammar sessions for repeat customers every day. I often felt that I couldn't say no to them, however, and while I was on their time I should do whatever I can to ensure that their papers were solid. The result was that these students often felt that I enjoyed these types of sessions and kept coming back with longer, more difficult papers that they expected I would just go through and edit. Many times I wanted to give the student to another tutor because I found these types of sessions very unengaging and depleting of the student-tutor interaction that made the other sessions more enjoyable. When I became the editor as opposed to the tutor, I felt immediately detached from the session and communication was hindered.

I think that learning where to draw the line is a concept that tutors should learn to develop, not only because it can enhance the comfort and enjoyment of the tutor, but because it can prevent the connection between tutors and students from becoming cold and sterile. The problem is defining what is most conducive to the student's success. Should the tutor bite the bullet and become the editor for the sake of the student's immediate success, or find another means to appease them, thereby ensuring the pending success of the student on future papers? The subject is a difficult one, and due to the amount of time I had to devote to each session, I unfortunately often had to choose the former option. But when so many of the papers that ESL students brought to me were their final master's projects, it was hard for me to want to enhance their skills as writers given that this was the last paper they would be evaluated on in school.

Jerry raises at least three important questions with ethical implications: what is best for the writer when he wants editing (see Chapter 8), what is our responsibility to graduate-level writers who are under pressure from their professors to produce fluent English, and what is best for those writers who are working on their last projects in English?

Sometimes what a writer needs might very well be an editor, someone to help with correctness, someone who will submit the proofread draft back to the writer. A colleague from India, a professor from our Speech and Hearing faculty, will contact me regularly and ask for just that: a tutor who will work with him as an editor, who will point out his errors and help him make his sentences more stylistically polished. He finds this process of using an editor quite normal and natural. He makes all his own choices about stylistic revisions and appreciates any instances where the editor helps him find errors, though these instances have become rare. Are these graduate students Jerry is working with reaching the point where this sort of paid editing is appropriate? These are important issues to explore with a director, to determine the writer's need and to assess the writer's engagement in the error analysis process. There might not be a simple answer, but Jerry need not have struggled with this question alone, and need not have had his time monopolized by sessions that strained his good nature. His director would surely have been happy to ask a writer to work with someone new, for a change of pace and a fresh perspective.

- *Should we correct every error?* Research shows that certain writers do not benefit from lengthy explanations of the uses of direct and indirect articles, but can learn well from work with verbs.[1] Is it our job to go through a master's thesis and find every article that needs correction? Perhaps our expertise is being wasted in these instances, since any native speaker can give this kind of help. Perhaps, if articles are the main problems, the writer can seek the help of friends and work with verbs and the clear presentation of important ideas with the writing tutor.

- *If we suggest that the writer hire an editor, do we make an unfair assumption that he can afford it?* Some writers surely can, while others will struggle to make ends meet in a country where a cup of coffee might cost more than three meals at home. Paid editors do not come cheap, nor should they. So what economic assumptions are we making if we decide a writer should seek out an editor?

- *Is it true that the master's thesis might be the last written work this writer will ever do in English?* Like it or not, English is fast becoming *the* language used in international contexts (see Chapter 13), so unless the writer is going back to an insulated kind of work in the original language, the chances are good of having to write in English again, even if the writer does not anticipate doing so. This is not to dismiss the question, but rather to complicate it. The answers are not simple.

Maybe some of Jerry's issues can be resolved by hard-and-fast rules a writing center has in place. How much editing is allowed? How many times may a writer come back to work on the same piece? These rules may make a decision easy but not necessarily optimal. Is it time to revisit these rules, to test them? Is it time to discuss them with the people who make them to see if the rules have some give? Is it time the rules were changed to accommodate writers with serious needs?

Craig has a different take on helping students with their English grammar:

> I have tutored many ESL students, and not only do I believe their individual needs fall under our job description, but I also believe these have been some of my most enjoyable sessions. While it is always rewarding to tutor a student on a more regular, thesis-driven paper, and see their ideas truly come together, I find an equal satisfaction in watching a student (often older) finally beginning to grasp the nuances of a language they are relatively new to. I believe

that we, as tutors, can be extremely helpful to ESL students, simply by taking the time to go through their papers focusing not only on conceptual points, but on its linguistic structure as well. This is extremely important, especially considering that our conceptual ideas are often constrained by our linguistic limitations; therefore, working to expand an ESL student's understanding of English, we are helping that student to develop their ability to create abstract ideas in English. By focusing on their lower-order concerns, we are able to raise them to a point where they can begin to write with . . . depth and understanding, to a point where they (and we as we tutor them) can focus on higher-order concerns. . . .

This talk may at times seem particularly arduous, but I feel it is our job. After all, we are getting paid to help students improve their writing, and if we have to spend a few hours looking at grammar and syntax and explaining basic sentence construction, then I believe we should be more than willing to do so, because these hours will most certainly improve an ESL student's ability to write well. It is our job to help students to improve their writing, and often this lower-order focus is necessary in order to provide the foundation on which students can really begin to develop their writing.

Craig has had positive experiences working with later-order concerns. Maybe the key difference between his experiences and Jerry's is that Jerry dealt with long and technically complex theses and felt he needed to work with the students together until they were finished or quit asking for help, while Craig does not mention the length of sessions or papers.

Tara has also faced a complicated situation with an ESL student:

A girl named Agnes came in with her textbook for a literature course on the Black Arts Movement [BAM]. Her assignment was to write the key points of three articles about major figures in the BAM. I asked Agnes if she had printed out a copy of her summary, and she said, "No, I haven't written it yet," at which point I asked what she would like to work on during our tutoring session. Agnes replied sheepishly, "Can you read the articles and help me understand them?" I had worked with Agnes before and knew her to be a Learning Assistance Center student who always put forth her best effort, but I wasn't sure if I was qualified or even obligated to be reading and explaining these articles. It was a slow day at the writing center, however, so I took the first article and began to read. I was able to understand the author's main points, and I read passages aloud and talked them over with Agnes, helping her to understand what the author meant. She was then able to write the first of the three summaries, so I left her to do that, but not without telling her first that writing center tutors were not really qualified to give her the kind of help she needed, and maybe she should talk to her professor or a reliable classmate for this kind of help in the future. Agnes has been back to the writing center since and we have continued to have fruitful sessions in which we deal with more appropriate issues in her writing assignments.

One tutor training guide, *The Allyn and Bacon Guide to Peer Tutoring*, contains an entire chapter called "Reading in the Writing Center." Clearly the authors believe that working with reading in the writing center is a legitimate way to spend time with a writer. The chapter summarizes the work of several reading theorists and suggests methods that help tutors avoid the problems associated with reading an article and providing the meaning for a writer. So instead, it makes suggestions the tutor can use to help the writer reflect on and develop a language to discuss her reading strategies. It suggests methods the tutor can use to model—and to discuss with the writer—successful approaches that might affect the writer's processes of reading. The book points out, for example, that a common strategy for poor readers is to reread the text that confuses them, but that "rereading won't be of much help if the vocabulary is unclear or if there's background information that the reader is missing or if the text is structured in a way that's unfamiliar to the reader."[2] It's certainly not only ESL writers who experience these kinds of reading challenges, and your center may have a policy about what you might do with a writer who has trouble comprehending the readings. In any case, it will be impossible for that writer to write well if the assignment requires a summary or analysis of the readings or an incorporation of written sources into the paper. Tara's experience shows how complex this situation is and how difficult it is if tutors are not prepared to work with writers who have reading roadblocks. In her narration of the previous session, Tara provided a welcoming session that gave the writer the help she needed immediately and that encouraged her to return to work on her writing. The writer learned to have a good feeling about asking for the help she needed.

Tara also narrates a happy resolution to another situation that tests those boundaries we've discussed:

Occasionally I have come across a student who seems to expect more than a normal tutoring session provides. This past semester a female student from Taiwan came to the writing center with a reflection paper about the first half of her college writing course. In the paper she discussed her feelings of isolation and inferiority after working alongside native speakers of English (including the professor) who would often cast aside her attempts to participate or simply fail to include her in class discussions. She talked about missing her mother and friends in Taiwan, and not being able to overcome the language barrier enough to make friends here in the United States. As I read the paper and spoke with the girl about points of grammar and organization, being as sensitive as I could about the delicate subject matter, I noticed she was crying. I realized then that I might have been the first person at IUP [Indiana University of Pennsylvania] to hear of her problems, and that while she did want help with grammar and transitions she also wanted someone to understand what she was saying and be kind to her as those in her classes had failed to do. We talked for a few minutes about her class and I asked if she had voiced her concerns to her professor privately and suggested that she do so. I also told her about the services and clubs that are available through the American Language Institute on campus, where many international students seem to be at home. She seemed much happier by the end of the session, and in addition to helping the girl solidify the structure of her paper I felt I also gave her a better sense of direction at our university. It is not the job of a writing center tutor to be a friend to lonely students, but knowing what it is to be away from home without the added stress of a language barrier I could not have taken any other course of action.

Later in the semester the girl came back with another paper and said she and her professor had become great friends and she spent much of her time with other international students. She seemed transformed, and I was glad to have helped her.

Tara is fortunate in that the writer has others on whom she can rely, and the university has services that are provided gladly by an organization for international students. Judith Powers points out that at times tutors act as cultural informants, and while she may be speaking primarily as an informant about the language the writer might use,[3] in this case Tara is acting as a valuable informant about the university's culture and services. And while she feels that it is not the job of the tutor to be the friend of an isolated, culture-shocked, and perhaps homesick young woman, it is her job to be kind and helpful.

But what would happen if IUP's American Language Institute did not exist? Tutors are strategically positioned to perceive and to evaluate student needs and university responses to those needs. Tutors and writing center directors together can be excellent advocates on campus and can make a powerful case that such a service is needed. Here is fertile ground for some research: How common is it for other schools to have such services? How are these services used on other campuses? How many students would use such an organization on your campus? If a paper is required for a peer tutor training course, perhaps a tutor could work with a trainee to write, research, and support such an argument and make sure the appropriate administrators—and faculty members, and perhaps students, through a student newspaper—got copies of it. Writing center tutors don't have to be passive consumers of academic policies; they can work, perhaps with the students who need these services, to make changes happen—changes for the better.

Sometimes it's clear that a writer's request is *not* our job, and we need to let the writer know. Cultural expectations about the tutorial interaction can put us in situations that make us uncomfortable. One such situation is when a writer assumes that our main purpose is to serve them. I remember a very demanding writer who found it incomprehensible that my schedule did not accommodate hers. She insisted on working only with me, but she also insisted that I make myself available when she could be on campus. I had to tell her that I had a schedule of obligations, too, and that I would be glad to meet with her during my available times. She had not been in this country long, and she had much to learn about the services offered to her on campus, that she could not be scolding or impolite if we did not satisfy her completely. We came to an understanding and worked together well, once we made our needs clear and listened to one another as equals.

It is never your job, because of cultural misunderstandings, to accept inappropriate staring, touching, or crowding. Excuse yourself immediately and let your director know promptly if such things go on, whether the writer is an ESL writer or not. It doesn't matter. These instances are rare, but can be very disturbing.

Perhaps the way you answer the questions about the limits of your job depends on the way you conceive of your work. Some literature on writing centers refers to tutors as professionals; this designation suggests that tutoring is a white-collar job, one in which issues and problems (such as the question, "Is this my job?") are dealt with using a team approach and creative brainstorming, perhaps along with your director, to conceive of fresh solutions to writing challenges. On the other hand, some literature, Nancy Grimm's book *Good Intentions: Writing Center Work for Postmodern Times,* for example, refers to "writing center workers," placing tutors in the ranks of the unionized labor force.[4] Beth Boquet has a chapter entitled "Tutoring as Hard Labor" in her book *Noise from the Writing Center.* Certainly anyone who has worked either on an assembly line or in a delivery room knows that this comparison is more metaphorical than literal, but Boquet makes interesting comparisons to both situations. Linda Shamoon and Deborah Burns' article "Labor Pains: A Political Analysis of Writing Center Tutoring" takes a neo-Marxist approach to writing centers and presents an argument that universities are "influenced by Fordist concepts of production, particularly the breaking apart of complex tasks into their simplest units of work in order to make possible large-scale production of easily reproducible parts, and the creating of easily filled slots for labor,"[5] They object to the "standardization of tutoring" in training manuals that set forth what they call a "low-skilled approach,"[6] a general set of instructions and a set of relatively inflexible methods for tutoring that assume that anyone, however modestly trained, can use to facilitate writing discussions.

How do these two polarities, these two extremes on a continuum, white collar and blue collar, help you to conceive of the questions raised in this chapter about the porous boundaries of that activity we refer to as your job? Do you conceive of yourself as a laborer working by the hour, tutoring by the book? Perhaps you think of your job as one that requires a solidarity of like-minded tutors who must struggle for fair working conditions and fair pay. Or perhaps you think of yourself as less a laborer and more a professional, working in a responsible role, making decisions for yourself. How do you set limits that maintain comfortable boundaries? Do you have the flexibility to set limits at all? How disposed are we to respond positively to some moving requests for help? (Writing center people tend to be very open and accepting, sometimes wanting to say yes when we should say no.) Staff meetings and other discussion forums with our peers and our directors are good places to bring up these questions, to raise them before we have to confront them with a writer who needs an answer right away, and to explore their complexities in ways that will benefit both writers and tutors alike.

The question "Is this my job?" is complex, and can be complicated when we find ourselves entering into the fun and excitement of knowing and working with interesting, intelligent people from other countries. These sessions, as Craig points out, can be among the most rewarding, most enjoyable work we do.

Notes

1. Chappell and Rodby (1983).

2. Gillespie and Lerner, 107.

3. Powers (1993).

4. Grimm (1999).

5. Shamoon and Burns, 63.

6. Shamoon and Burns, 65.

Works Cited

Boquet, Elizabeth. 2002. *Noise from the Writing Center*. Logan, UT: Utah State University Press.

Chappell, Virginia A., and Judith Rodby. 1983. "Verb Tense and ESL Composition: A Discourse Level Approach." In *On TESOL '82: Perspectives on Language Learning and Teaching,* edited by Mark A. Clarke and Jean Handscombe, 309–20. Washington, DC: TESOL.

Gillespie, Paula, and Neal Lerner. 2004. *The Allyn and Bacon Guide to Peer Tutoring.* 2d ed. New York: Pearson Longman.

Grimm, Nancy. 1999. *Good Intentions: Writing Center Work for Postmodern Times.* Portsmouth, NH: Boynton/Cook.

Powers, Judith K. 1993 "Rethinking Writing Center Conferencing Strategies for the ESL Writer." *The Writing Center Journal* 13 (2): 39–48.

Shamoon, Linda, and Deborah Burns. 2001. "Labor Pains: A Political Analysis of Writing Center Tutoring." In *The Politics of Writing Centers*, edited by Jane Nelson and Kathy Evertz, 62–73. Portsmouth, NH: Boynton/Cook.

12

Creative Writing Workshops for ESL Writers

Kevin Dvorak

Up to this point, the chapters in this part of the book have offered strategies for tutors to implement during their tutoring sessions. This chapter, however, does something a little different; it offers ideas for creative writing workshops that are specifically designed for English as a second language (ESL) writers and how your writing center can facilitate them. These workshops differ from familiar workshops in that they focus primarily on the act of creation, rather than requiring students to bring in works they have already written. I offer a rationale for incorporating these workshops for ESL writers in writing centers, provide examples of workshop activities, and show how to get them started.

Writing as the Center of Activities

Creative writing is too often an overlooked and undervalued form of literacy learning in the academy, especially when it pertains to learning English as a second language (ESL). Most contexts in which ESL students use English outside of the academy are less formal and more creative than those they use in classrooms; however, academic instructors do not ask these writers to cross the lines between academic composition and informal, creative writing as often as they should.[1] Instructors should be inviting ESL students to cross these lines more than they do because creative writing benefits all language users by encouraging writers to express themselves in more creative and colloquial terms, ways nonnative speakers are more likely to hear and speak English when not in classrooms. Experiences with creative writing—as writers, readers, or listeners— enhance ESL writers' linguistic and cognitive experiences with English, thereby helping them better understand their worlds through English.[2]

As writing center practitioners, we often do not tutor ESL writers in creative ways of expression—but we can change this. We can place ourselves in a unique position to affect the literacy development of ESL writers by offering them something few classes do: opportunities to write creatively. Since writing centers are commonly nonauthoritative, cosmopolitan hubs where students come together to interact with each other's ideas and written languages, they are prime locations for ESL writers to develop these types of writing abilities. By offering creative writing workshops to ESL writers, writing centers become gathering spots for various language users as they

- promote writing as a fun activity—fun that is often overlooked when trying to compose pressure-filled, academic, formal prose
- create an environment where nonnative speakers interact with tutors in literacy activities
- encourage ESL writers to take risks while writing—risks they may feel intimidated to take in academic writings
- engage ESL writers in writings that are "constructed around the unique," which provide individuals with better understandings of who they are and how they fit into particular social situations[3]

I believe providing this type of atmosphere is a fantastic opportunity for both ESL writers and tutors to experience diversity development. The risks involved, the conversations and readings involved, and the fun that surrounds them, all combine to offer ESL students the experiences they usually do not receive in classrooms but that they need for personal growth.

Releasing Writers into English

By *creative writing workshop*, I do not mean a text-centered workshop where students bring in drafts of creative writings they have already written. Instead, I emphasize the middle word in this expression: *writing*. These are creative *writing* workshops, workshops that are centered around the act of writing. By *creative*, I mean that ESL writers should write prompted writes and freewrites that produce stories, poetry, short fictional scenes—anything that implies "creativity" beyond academic writing. By *writing*, I mean the actual act of writing, pen(cil)-to-paper, finger-to-keyboard-to-monitor. By *workshop*, I mean an interactive, social environment where writings are produced and shared in an encouraging community setting. In all, these workshops offer ESL writers opportunities to visit writing centers to engage in freewriting writing activities.

- *Tip:* The facilitator should make it clear to the participants that these acts of writing are, essentially, acts of freewriting. In fact, it may help to clarify the following three points about freewrites:
  1. They are not revised or refined.
  2. They have not gone through the whole writing process as we usually define it.
  3. They are supposed to sound rough.

There are hundreds of writing activities that can be used in a creative writing workshop. Many writing activities you've experienced can be used outright or modified. One of the best things about these activities is that they can be manipulated so that a group may engage in the same general tasks, but in ways that vary enough from one another that they do not appear the same.[4] First, let's look at some activities you can do in a creative writing workshop and, then, we'll see how to set up the workshop itself.

Activity One: Basic Collaborative Fiction Write-Around[5]

This write-around can serve as a creative way for participants to introduce themselves by allowing ESL writers to create fictional scenes, images, and identities about themselves and the worlds around them. Writers begin by writing a fictional narrative about themselves. If it helps, writers can be given the following opening to begin with: "I am _____ _____ and I am from _____."
Writers should then write for a few minutes, until the facilitator announces when one minute remains. When time is up, have the writers pass their writings to one side so that each writer has another author's writing. Have each writer read her new passage quickly and continue where the previous author stopped. (It may even be fun to allow each writer to read only a few of the just-written lines of her new work before writing.) While writing, writers should be encouraged to add dialogue, scenery, concrete images, even a word written in their native language—anything that will add to their uniqueness.

- *Tip:* Play along. This is a learning experience for everyone. Every participant has a role in the creation of this atmosphere. Everyone is a writer, a reader, and a listener. And always provide specific instructions before starting each activity.

Activity Two: Prompted Quick-Writes

A second activity is freewriting from prompts. Prompts can be found almost anywhere, from books about creative writing to asking someone to call out a prompt and having each writer write about it for a few minutes. Another way is to have each writer write a prompt on a small piece of paper, put them all into a bowl, and then, either have each writer pick one prompt from the bowl and write from it, or pick single prompts from the bowl and have everyone write from them. These freewrites should be quick. By writing one after another, writers are challenged to shift ways of thinking quickly and to take their thoughts in new directions.

- *Variation:* Instead of quick-writes, students can write poems from the prompts. This encourages ESL writers to use English in many nontraditional ways.

Activity Three: Picture This

Another activity is writing from pictures. Bring a variety of pictures to the workshop: from magazines, newspapers, catalogues, family photo albums, and so on. Or, have writers bring pictures from their own cultures, and make this a fun way to explore multicultural perspectives. Pass them around and have the writers construct stories about the photos they receive. By looking at photos of other people's lives and creating scenes around them, writers can situate themselves in comparison to others.

- *Variation:* Either the stories or photos can be passed around at intervals. (See Activity One or Two as a guide.)

Activity Four: A Portrait of the Writer (Guided Self-Portraits)[6]

This activity allows writers to construct their identities in a variety of ways, something international students will already have some experience with. Create a number of sentence-level prompts that will build on one another in an effort to construct a paragraph (or more) about someone or something. For example, three consecutive sentence-opening prompts could be: "I was walking . . ."; "And then I found . . ."; "But, before I could . . . ." Or, a facilitator could follow Wendy Bishop's guidelines from *Released into Language*. Where Bishop asks writers to think of a person they want to write about, choose a title for their piece, begin with an opening sentence, and follow with sentences that focus on using descriptive language, such as Write a sentence with a color in it; Write a sentence with a body part in it; Write a sentence with a smell and a color in it.[7]

- *Variation:* This game can be played as another write-around, this time constructing a letter to someone (especially funny if it is to another participant). The first person begins the letter with a greeting ("Dear _____," "Hey _____!" or "Yo _____!"). Then, fold the paper over to cover the writing and pass it to one side, where the next writer opens the letter. These could be the first three prompts of a progression: "I saw you . . . "; But you were . . . "; "And now we are. . . . " The last writer should close with a salutation.

Facilitating Creative Writing Workshops for ESL Writers

Now that you know some of the activities, it is time to organize them into workshops. The following is a quick, three-step process that will take you from how to organize a workshop to facilitating one once it has started.

- Step One: Choosing a Facilitator

The first step in facilitating a creative writing workshop for ESL writers is deciding who the facilitator is going to be. I suggest it be run by tutors—anything to get away from potential authority figures—who have interests in both teaching ESL writers and working with creative writing. Facilitators could also include one student interested in ESL pedagogy and another in creative writing pedagogy.

- Step Two: Build It and Writers Will Write

After deciding who is going to facilitate the workshop, the facilitator needs to determine who is going to be asked to participate. The following are a few key questions that will need to be answered: Will only first-year ESL students be invited? Will upper-level and graduate ESL writers be invited? How will the workshop be advertised?

- *Tip:* I hazard a caution about having writers whose first language is English participate in these workshops. First, this is a celebration of ESL writers writing creatively. Second, due to the workshop's emphasis on audience participation, I would not want ESL writers to feel intimidated by L1 writers who are more familiar with English.[8] If writers are going to be asked to read aloud, they should feel comfortable about it: before, during, and after reading.

- Step Three: Timing the Whole, Timing Activities

Before beginning a workshop, the facilitator should set a specific length of time for the whole workshop—usually between forty-five and ninety minutes—and for each activity. Here lies a crucial situation: not letting the whole workshop or any one activity last too long. Keeping activities short keeps writers engaged.

So, how much time an activity gets depends on the activity and the judgment of the facilitator. For example, I think no freewrite should last more than ten minutes. Allot five minutes after that to allow students to read and you have an activity that lasts around fifteen minutes. Some activities involve more interactive writing and may last longer. The length of reading sessions will also vary with the number of participants, how many are willing to read aloud, and how long the writings are.

- *Tip:* Use time effectively; downtime, when many are not reading, writing, or listening, can cause writers to lose attentiveness. If writers feel they want more time, encourage them to write more outside of the workshop and bring it to the next workshop to share.

When creative writings have been community created, as described by the previous activities, they can be fun to write, read, and listen to because they are not sole products of one person but of a community of learners, of writers working together to have fun while engaging in acts of literacy.

Experiencing creative writing in the United States allows ESL writers to engage in the many layers of English other than the academic, thus enabling them to better understand and experience their worlds through English.[9] Providing creative writing workshops to ESL writers helps writing centers add to the diversity of experiences ESL writers have with English, to the diversity of experiences tutors have with ESL students, and to the diversity of literacy practices writing centers promote.

Notes

1. Bishop (1994).
2. Hanauer (2003).
3. Hanauer, 79.

4. I could go on describing prompts for an entire book; however, I'd prefer referring to a few creative writing books as guides:
   - *Madlibs*
   - Susan Woolridge, *Poem Crazy* (1996)
   - Wendy Bishop, *Released into Language* (1990)

5. See Bishop (1990), 117, for another version of this activity.

6. Bishop (1990), 98. For this activity, Bishop offers a fifteen-sentence guide to construct a descriptive paragraph.

7. Bishop (1990), 99.

8. Here, we should consider Matsuda's and Cox's concern about having ESL writers read aloud. (See Chapter 4.)

9. Hanauer, 71.

Works Cited

Bishop, Wendy. 1990. *Released into Language: Options for Teaching Creative Writing.* Urbana, IL: NCTE.

_____. 1994. "Crossing the Lines: On Creative Composition and Composing Creative Writing." In *Colors of a Different Horse: Rethinking Creative Writing Theory and Pedagogy*, edited by Wendy Bishop and Hans Ostrom, 181–97. Urbana, IL: NCTE.

Hanauer, David Ian. 2003. "Multicultural Moments in Poetry: The Importance of the Unique," *The Canadian Modern Language Review* 60: 69–87.

13

The Role of Writing in Higher Education Abroad

Gerd Bräuer

The Situation

Imagine this: A student who grew up in Germany comes to your writing center to get help with his first paper he has to prepare for a class. The paper is already done, and he just wants to drop it off to be edited as soon as possible. After you tell him that tutoring writing doesn't work like this and that he would have to make an appointment to actually work *together with a tutor* on his paper, he gets rather upset and is ready to leave.

Another situation: A student who went to school in Russia sits in your tutoring session and wants to talk about the correct usage of grammar in her paper. Nevertheless, after you glanced over her paper, you are convinced that this text first needs a major structural revision and that any correction of linguistic errors should be left for later. Even though this student stays for the rest of the session, questions about grammar and spelling come up almost every minute, and you can tell that her mind is *not* focused on structural revision.

And a third scene to be imagined: A student who just arrived from his native country, China, comes to you for help. Like the students in the other two cases, he also wants to have his paper edited, but he readily agrees when you suggest to him to work on the focus of his paper first. During the session, you wonder why he keeps nodding even when you ask questions about what he wanted to say in a specific paragraph. You don't know what to make of his smiles when you eventually come forward with your own interpretation of what he is trying to say in his paper. But you certainly become suspicious about his nodding again when you suggest structural changes. When the session is over you realize that you did all the talking and revising yourself. Nevertheless, this student seems very pleased with your work.

The Problem

Even though the educational cultures these students grew up with are probably very different from one another, all three examples show significant similarities in two aspects:

- The students have a specific understanding of the role of the tutor as either editor or teacher. With this in mind, and now being confronted with a rather different function of tutoring, they either get upset and leave the writing center or (mostly subconsciously) try to manipulate the tutor to fit their expectations.

- The students envision text feedback as something done only after they have finished writing and as surface editing mainly in regard to spelling and grammar.

From my own experience with international student writers in Germany, the Czech Republic, international summer schools in various countries, and different U.S. universities over the past fifteen years, there seems to be a third similarity among second language writers, which I have not portrayed in my examples: That of *not coming* to the writing center at all. An international student, who, out of despair that she could finish her BA thesis in time, eventually sought help during her last semester of study from the writing center I started in 2001 at the University of Education in Freiburg, Germany. When I asked her why she didn't come earlier, she wrote this:

> For a long time, I simply didn't know that there is a writing center at the university. Then, when someone pointed it out to me, I kept asking myself what a writing center actually is and does. When I finally had the guts to ask my academic advisor, I heard from him that you discuss your manuscripts with a writing tutor. For a long time, I felt too embarrassed to actually do it. I kept telling myself: What would we talk about? I don't have anything interesting to say in my papers. And help with grammar I can get from my (. . .) friends.

Reason One for the Problem: The Role of Writing in Higher Education

At some point, U.S. tutors may wonder how their ESL students are accustomed to working with writing center tutors in their home countries, and whether writing instruction abroad is the same as it is in the United States. These questions are important to answer because U.S. tutors may gain a greater understanding of the ways ESL students' writing experiences in their home countries affect their tutoring sessions in U.S. writing centers.

Outside of Anglo-American higher education, the idea of writing centers and peer tutoring that goes beyond helping with grammar is still very new, or, in other words, there are only a few university writing centers in the non-English-speaking world. In Europe, for example, interest in writing support has started to develop only since the early 1990s. The Academic Writing Center at the University of Copenhagen, Denmark, founded in 1992, and the Writing Lab at the University of Bielefeld, Germany, two years later, were among the first ones, when Western European universities began to adopt the Anglo-American credit system and to develop BA and MA programs compatible with those in the English-speaking countries. This move is intended to attract more international students to study in Europe. Along with these new programs came the pressure (mostly financial) to shorten study time—usually four years for a BA and two years for an MA. This is something that previously had been unknown to most European universities where students often stay several more years to finish their degrees. With this limitation of study time, there emerged an immediate need for extracurricular support for the students, which has been given to them at some universities through so-called study support centers and, in other cases, through writing centers.

Nevertheless, until a few years ago, the existence of these centers did not mean a change in the role of writing in higher education. As for many decades, students would use writing mostly for notetaking in class, to prepare oral presentations (usually one per seminar and semester), for exams and long semester papers and, at the end of their study, for a degree thesis. *Documenting* and *presenting* knowledge were (and still are in many universities) the major functions of writing. Some students may be discussing early drafts of their papers among themselves, but usually they work alone until they hand in their work. From the instructor, students receive a grade and sometimes a few, but often no, comments on their written performance.[1] As a result of this situation and the fact that academic writing has not been taught in most European universities, many students give up (some say about 50 percent of all college dropouts in Germany leave because of major writing problems) after sometimes years of desperately trying to find out how to put together academic papers in a satisfying manner.

With the growing international reputation of U.S. writing pedagogy, things are slowly starting to change with regard to the role of writing, at least at Western European universities. Even though there has been research on the writing process in countries like Germany for years,[2] institutional consequences on a large scale, drawn out of research and theories about the nature of writing, began to appear only as a result of the curricular reform I mentioned earlier toward BA and MA programs and the urgent search of administrators for study support. Now at almost every university in Germany there are workshops providing an introduction to process writing and to the specifics of academic writing. Nevertheless, these workshops are not mandatory and in many cases are offered just once each semester. Given the small number of workshops and their voluntary character, my estimate is that only about 5 percent of the student population participates. As a result, aspects of process writing such as prewriting, drafting, peer feedback, revision, and editing are still not mainstream and, if in existence at all, their efficiency will, most of the time, neither be reflected upon nor evaluated. Things like learning logs and writing portfolios are still widely unknown. Therefore, the consciousness of being (or becoming) a writer who is able to grow if he makes use of the resources of the writer's community is still underdeveloped at least among students at German universities. Just from my work with students from other countries during the past decade, this seems to be the case also in other educational cultures that rely heavily on the idea of writing as documenting and presenting knowledge, excluding the other functions of writing such as the *reflection, transformation,* and *development* of knowledge.

Reason Two for the Problem: Rhetorical Traditions

In the first book about writing centers and writing programs in Europe, Rienecker and Jörgensen introduce an interesting distinction between what they call the "Anglo-American" and the "Continental" way of writing,[3] with the Anglo-American way being more systematic and "caring" toward the reader, making sure at any point in the text the reader would be able to follow the line of argument by, what I call, *reproducing* the text. We all know the extreme version of this style of writing: the five-paragraph essay. In contrast, the Continental way of writing is not systematic in a way that the reader would be able to predict the development of the argument from the beginning of the text. It is expected that the reader *co-produces*, so to speak, the text by puzzling together the various argumentative aspects the writer has to offer. Whereas the Anglo-American mode of writing would deliver the major thesis of a text, its Continental counterpart expects the reader, in ever narrowing hermeneutic circles, to unfold the major thesis of the text herself.

While this distinction is indeed a very theoretical one, because we all know writers of the Anglo-American world that write excellent Continental-style texts, and Continental writers practicing a superb Anglo-American style, still it is important for ESL tutors to know about the fact that there *are* different traditions in the practice of rhetoric. Even though we may not know the details of the tradition that have influenced a certain ESL writer throughout his/her educational upbringing, we need to *acknowledge* and *honor* the existence of these cultural roots. This can easily be done during the tutoring session by showing interest in the way of writing that the ESL student is accustomed. We need to make clear that learning how to compose texts in a second language does *not* mean having to give up one's native writing traditions. Nevertheless, it is sometimes easier for the writer to make progress in mastering the linguistic aspects of the newly learned language by focusing on a rather simple yet self-explaining or referential style such as the Anglo-American, and to try to incorporate aspects of his native style of writing later on, when the linguistic concerns are felt to be less cumbersome. Another necessity for getting acquainted with the writing tradition of a second language is the fact that many readers of this language often rely on the patterns of their native writing tradition in order to understand fully what is being said in a text.

Reason Three for the Problem: The Faculty

In order to understand fully what makes many ESL students act differently than their American peers when it comes to working on their texts, we have to take a separate look at the faculty whom ESL students experience in their home countries. In Germany, and I assume this is true for quite a number of other educational cultures, many faculty have little knowledge about writing pedagogy, and they don't consciously reflect on their own writing process. As they experienced as students themselves, they take for granted that one learns how to write in grade school and if there would be any need for writing support at the university at all, this would have to be covered by the first language department. It is widely unknown that the process of learning how to write never really ends in a writer's lifetime, especially when she enters new discursive communities such as in freshman year, or when students start specializing in their major discipline.

Most faculty are familiar neither with what in the United States is called "writing across the curriculum" nor with "writing in the disciplines." As a result, outside of the first language departments, little to no attention is paid to the quality of text, with the possible exception of issues of grammar and spelling. Therefore, most of the time, students don't get any hints as to why they did poorly on their papers. This, unfortunately, lets them think that the reason for their failure is a lack of knowledge in their discipline. Even though there certainly is a strong connection between clarity of thought and language, these students seldom realize that they could in fact gain clarity in their ideas through *developing* them in writing. This is no wonder, because to use writing as a tool for learning is rarely encouraged by the faculty. Techniques like brainstorming, clustering, freewriting, or mind-mapping, that do promote thinking, have just recently found their way into primary and secondary education, less, though, into college and university. Watching their college instructor, students get the impression that he is a *genius*, writing articles and books and never having any writing problems.

At least this is the image presented by many faculty at universities in Germany. They don't share with students their lives as writers who also experience the daily struggle of getting the right words on paper. They don't encourage students to come forward with their writing problems. All in all, everyone ends up believing that whoever struggles with writing doesn't belong at the university. Therefore, when many students go abroad and start writing in another language, they continue to think that composing a text successfully is all about disciplinary knowledge, second language problems excluded. For the latter they would seek someone who can help edit the final draft. It is beyond the imagination of many that peer tutors, who don't even belong to the same discipline, would be able to comment on their drafts in any helpful way.

A Few Suggestions for How to Deal with the Problem

What can be done at American writing centers to make the tutoring of ESL writers more efficient? The effort should start long before the actual tutoring session takes place. Writing tutors could support writing center administrators and faculty with the following aspects:

- Advertise broadly on campus not only the existence, but also the kind of work a writing center is doing. Make sure to point out the differences between tutoring writing (the concern is focused on the development of writer *and* text) and editing (the concern is focused only on the text). Tell ESL students that their previous experience as a first language writer matters greatly as a springboard for successful second language writing.

- Provide incoming students with information sessions about the process character of writing and the importance of feedback throughout the development of texts. Show them the specific nature of peer tutoring and what sets this kind of interaction apart from conferences with the instructor. Let ESL students know that their culturally coined expectations about how to deal with their drafts are being considered in the writing center.

- Publicize outstanding results of student writing that profited from the interaction with the writing center. Don't forget to include ESL texts as well as texts in foreign languages written by students whose first language is English to demonstrate that *everyone* can improve as a writer.

- Make sure to underline the potential your writing center has for the shaping of a distinct ESL writers' community on campus where students will learn how to interact with each other as writers in a constructive and supporting way. (See Chapter 12.)

All of these aspects are necessary to be communicated to native language writers as well. Nevertheless, you should consider going the extra mile to reach out to ESL writers:

- Provide material about the writing center in an informational packet given to new students so they can familiarize themselves with the university writing center before they actually arrive on campus. This will help them direct their expectations about becoming a writer in college at an early stage.

- Collaborate closely with the ESL faculty to ensure that students will be sent to the writing center as part of fulfilling their writing assignments. This will help them to remember reflective practice and text feedback as common aspects of their daily writing routine.

In order to learn more about different cultures of writing and dealing with writers and their texts, I suggest you collaborate with international writing tutors and share your experience and expertise. For example, you can get in touch with writing tutors from the University of Education in Freiburg, Germany, who go through a four-semester certification program before they start working for the writing center. To learn more about your peers in Freiburg, visit their website at *www.ph-freiburg.de/schreibzentrum* or contact them at *schreibzentrum@ph-freiburg.de*. I would like to encourage you to write them about your personal experience in tutoring ESL writers. Tell them about your successful strategies, ask questions, and express your doubts. Ask them about the tutoring strategies they prefer. Invite them to contact you for advice when they run into problems with American students abroad. I am convinced that there will be a lot to learn from each other.

Notes

1. See Foster and Russell (2002) for a more in-depth analysis of academic writing in higher education in Germany and other countries.
2. Antos and Pogner (1995) and Merz-Grötsch (2000).
3. Rienecker and Jörgensen, 102–103.

Works Cited

Antos, G., and K.–H. Pogner. 1995. *Schreiben*. Reihe: Studienbibliographien Sprachwissenschaft. Heidelberg: Groos.

Björk, Lennart A., Gerd Bräuer, Lotte Rienecker, and Peter Stray Jörgensen, eds. 2003. *Teaching Academic Writing in European Higher Education*. Amsterdam: Kluwer Academic Publishers.

Foster, David, and David Russell. 2002. *Writing and Learning in Cross-National Perspective: Transitions from Secondary to Higher Education*. Urbana, IL: NCTE.

Merz-Grötsch, J. 2000. *Schreiben als System* (Vol. 1). Freiburg, i.Br.: Fillibach.

Rienecker, Lotte, and Peter Stray Jörgensen. 2003. "The (Im)possibilities in Teaching University Writing in the Anglo-American Tradition When Dealing with Continental Student Writers." In *Teaching Academic Writing in European Higher Education*, edited by L. Bjork, G. Bräuer, L. Rienecker, and P. Jörgensen, 101–12. Amsterdam: Kluwer Academic Publishers.

14

Trying to Explain English

Ben Rafoth

By some estimates, English is used by roughly one in six people on earth, either as a mother tongue or a second language. It is the *lingua franca* for much of the world's trade, media, and e-commerce.[1] In India and some African countries, it is the mother tongue for many people as well as their nation's official language, as in Nigeria and Zimbabwe. Even in countries where English is not the national or predominant language, it is often incorporated into existing languages, giving us Deutschlish in Germany, for example, as well as Franglais in France, Singlish in Singapore, and Swinglish in Sweden.

With so many varieties, English means different things to different people, and it thrives in an array of forms with hybrid vocabularies, multiple levels of formality, and a myriad of accents. Students who visit the United States to study in colleges and universities often have had a good deal of exposure to English in their own countries, though not necessarily to any variety of the language we would recognize. They may bring with them a mixture of truly international exposures to the language gathered from multilingual teachers, Hollywood movies, and Hong Kong shopping trips. And when they land in the United States, they will find that English in the States is as diverse as the population itself, from the border towns of Texas to the hills of Appalachia. By contrast, for many teachers and tutors in the United States, there are not multiple Englishes but only one English: Standard American English (SAE). As native speakers, most of us do not know what it is like to learn English in a non-English country from many different sources. We learned English in the relatively closed environments of our family and neighborhood communities. As children, we skated right through all of its irregular verbs, collocations, and crazy compounds. And for this reason, we would do well to pause now and then to reflect on some aspects of learning English that we take for granted as native speakers but prove difficult for new learners.

In this chapter, I invite you to take a stroll along a few linguistic paths through the gardens of English grammar so that we can reflect on some of the

140

reasons why learning English seems so easy for native speakers and so challenging for those who are learning it as a second language. Along the way, I hope to point out a few facts about the language we ought to keep in mind when we help English as a Second Language (ESL) students. We tend to shun discussions of grammar, except to remind ourselves that tutors are not proofreaders and our centers are not grammar fix-it shops, and we tell ourselves that learning grammar doesn't help writers anyway. I don't want to go down that road, but in any case, I am not referring to grammar-as-surface-correctness. I am referring to the way English is put together, the shape of its Lego Blocks and how they got that way. We can welcome ESL students into our writing centers, but that is not enough. We must also make an effort to understand English from a linguistic perspective and prepare ourselves to pass this information on to the students we tutor. By accepting this challenge, we will provide them with the keys that will help unlock the linguistic doors of their new language.

A Flimsy Jacket Versus a Jacket That Is Flimsy

Native speakers of English can have difficulty explaining why it is correct to say something one way and not another. This can be frustrating when an international student in your writing center, trying to correct an error, asks you to explain why, for example, adjectives cannot follow nouns as they do in many other languages. Sometimes it's easy. Tutors usually know, for example, that adjectives pitch their tents before nouns or after linking verbs, as in *the flimsy jacket* or *the jacket is flimsy*, but they cannot follow nouns as in *jacket flimsy*. You could probably explain this to your ESL student by pointing to the nouns, verbs, and adjectives in a sentence and then stating a general rule based on these examples. For example: Adjectives can go either before nouns or after linking verbs like *is* or *seems*.

But just when you think you have this rule figured out, you discover that some adjectives refuse to be seen with verbs. This is why we can say *the previous class* but not *the class is previous*. Why, after all, can we say *the jacket is flimsy* but not *the class is previous*? If you were asked this question by an ESL student and are like most tutors, you might be just as perplexed as your tutee, and you wouldn't be the first to scratch your head and reply, "Uhm, that's just the way we say it." As you continue to think about this aspect of English on the way to your next class, you might decide that *previous* and perhaps a few other words like it are just flukes. But things get even flukier: Some adjectives behave the opposite of *previous* and they refuse to associate with nouns: a deck can be awash but it cannot be an awash deck. Soldiers can stand abreast but they cannot be abreast soldiers. So, something as outwardly simple as putting adjectives together with nouns masks an inner complexity that can be befuddling to ESL students and isn't much clearer to the rest of us. While tutors know how to use words like *flimsy*, *previous*, *awash*, and *abreast*, explaining the rules that govern these words to ESL students can be maddening. This

example helps to make the point of this chapter—we can all benefit from thinking about what makes English challenging to learn as a second language.

Not a Particularly Difficult Language to Learn

One thing we can rule out right off the bat is any notion that English is a harder
language to learn than most others. This may come as disappointing news to
some people who think English is supposed to be difficult. Perhaps they enter-
tain a fantasy that English is uniquely inscrutable, believing it confers a special
degree of conceptual richness not shared by other languages. Or perhaps like
many cultures throughout time, they regard their language with deep pride and
believe it brings them strength and power—an admirable sentiment. The truth
is that every language is unique and loathes to give up its secrets to anyone but
its native speakers. Children the world over learn their native languages at
about the same rate, and by age 6 or 7 have mastered its basic structure. Then
once we reach puberty and the magical moment is over, our brains start to close
the gate, and to get in, *you have to pay*.

The degree to which learning any language—English, Korean, or some
other—is more difficult than learning another is a question linguists have pon-
dered. The consensus is that no language is more difficult than another in an
absolute sense. But in a relative sense, yes—if English is your native language
then it is easier to learn Dutch, German, or other Germanic languages than to
learn, say, a Turkic language like Kazakh or Tatar, or a Bantu language like
Zulu or Xhosa.[2] (See Chapter 2.) Similarly, it is easier for a Swede to learn
Norwegian than Polish, and easier for a Czech to learn Polish than Norwegian.
"The major reason for this," explains one linguist, "is that the vocabularies
have so many similarities in both form and content in the related languages."[3]
This assumes, naturally, that all other things are equal, and they rarely are. If
you have traveled extensively in another country, spent time with relatives who
speak the language, or enjoy some other advantage, the task can be significantly easier for you. On the other hand, if you are stuck in a strange and far-
away country, feel homesick, and dread the food, you may not be terribly motivated to pick up the new language and may even resist it until you can resolve
these feelings. The ease or difficulty of learning any language, then, is always
more about the learners than the language.

With more than 500,000 words in the most comprehensive dictionaries,
English does have an exceptionally large lexicon. One could argue that this fact
alone makes English harder to learn than languages with far fewer words. But
consider this question: Is it easier to express your thoughts in a language with a
large lexicon or a small one? With lots of words to choose from, it may be easier to choose among multiple ways to express a thought, or to rephrase an
expression for someone who does not understand. Besides, even if there are
many words to learn in a language, this does not mean that a language with
fewer words is necessarily any easier. There is a verb in Nootka, an American

Indian language, for instance, that means "I have been accustomed to eat twenty round objects while engaged in . . . . " The structure of Nootka verbs is quite complex, and the language's relatively small vocabulary does not make up for the difficulty of learning Nootka verbs. Or consider the fact that the average American high school graduate has a vocabulary not of 500,000 words but of 45,000 to 60,000 words.[4] Similarly, carpenters, airplane mechanics, and chefs may not always have the most advanced university degrees, but they have quite extensive technical vocabularies. In other words, the number of words in the dictionary is not nearly as important as knowing the ones you need to know to get along in the culture, to work there, or to pass your college's proficiency test.

A Gift from Foreigners

English's large vocabulary is in fact a point of pride, but the reason for this is largely historical, and we have foreigners to thank for much of it. Roman merchants and Christian missionaries brought many Latin words into Old English during the first millennium. Then in 1066, the invader William the Conqueror and his armies catapulted hundreds of words into English from the Norman dialect of French. Before 1066, for example, the Anglo-Saxons had only the word *king* to express ideas about anything that was kingly. But after the Norman invasion, English gained the synonyms *royal, regal,* and *sovereign.* It may be said that the House of English was a mere hut before the foreign-born words took up residence but a castle afterward, as McCrum exemplifies in word groups like *rise-mount-ascend, ask-question-interrogate,* or *time-age-epoch.*[5] Today, a thousand years later, English is still adding wings onto the castle, thanks to the constant influx of new words from cultures around the world that have enriched the language beyond measure: *reggae, liaison, gestalt, ciao, chic, passé, mojo, juggernaut, pundit,* and *heebie jeebies.* The worldwide music and entertainment industries serve to transmit words from a variety of cultures into songs and movie scripts heard around the world. The English lexicon grows with words even from alien life forms (*tribble, muggles, borg,* and *hobbit*).

If foreigners have given us thousands of new words, they have not made us spell them the way we do. We have inflicted that pain entirely on ourselves. No discussion of the challenges of learning English would be complete without mentioning the enigma of the English spelling system. It's so bad, George Bernard Shaw pointed out, he could spell *fish* as *ghoti*: *gh* from tough, *o* from women, and *ti* from nation. English spelling evolved over centuries and settled down into fixed forms somewhat haphazardly around the time of the printing press and thereafter. Noah Webster tried to regularize spelling, and we owe him for helping with at least some of our more commonsense spellings. He regularized *tyre* to *tire* and *fibre* to *fiber,* among others. But the number of words in print even during Webster's time was enormous, and he could only do so much. He left untouched, for example, the thirteen different ways we have of spelling the *sh* sound: *shoe, sugar, issue, mansion, mission, nation, suspicion, ocean, conscious*, *chaperon*, *schist*, *fuchsia*, and *pshaw*.[6] If there is any consolation in the chaos of English spelling, it is that the way we pronounce words and the way we spell them can never be matched up for very long. Pronunciation is forever the wanderer, while spellings are homebound. Pronunciation is restless and shuns commitment; spelling is sedentary and dedicated. We could change tomorrow all the spellings to fit the way we talk. In a few hundred years, maybe less, we would all look back and wonder why we ever wasted our time trying to reform a relationship that was meant to be on the rocks. Meanwhile, for some ESL learners as for the rest of us—and flawed though it is—there is spell-check.

There are other aspects of English that make it both a curse and a blessing for new learners. While there are only about 180 irregular verbs, for example, many of them occur often. They don't follow much of a pattern (could this be why we call them irregular?) and they have to be memorized, like *went*, *shut*, *heard*, and *flew*. Some languages have far more irregular forms, and while ESL learners may make errors with verb forms, when it comes to writing they are like many native speakers of the language and often have the most trouble with verb endings, prepositions, and agreement. One reason for this is that these are features of the language that often convey little meaning. We could lose many verb endings and hardly miss them, not to mention agreement between pronouns and their antecedents and subjects and verbs. On the other hand, prepositions are essential to English but they're fickle. Does it matter whether we ride in a boat or on it? Walk in the door or through it? No. Yet English insists that we lie *in* bed but *on* the couch.[7] So when we find ourselves or our ESL students struggling with these features of English, perhaps it is some consolation to remember that they may not be all that important in the first place. In fact, let's embrace the learner dialects of our ESL writers and simply agree that, so long as the meaning is clear, it is okay to overlook prepositions and articles used in nonstandard ways (see Chapters 3 and 6). This would have the added benefit of taking a lot of our native English-speaking students off the hook, too.

English is quite flexible in its ability to convert verbs to nouns to adjectives, as in *fly-flight-flighty*. One might imagine ESL learners would welcome such fluidity because the words are so closely related in form and meaning. Or are they? If you know the meaning of *corn*, does that help when you encounter the word *corny*? How about *horn* and *horny*? *Hip* and *hippie*? English can be amusing and treacherous at the same time. Does *flighty* describe someone who flies on an airplane flight? Does *weighty* describe something whose weight is weighed? No, silly. But that's the point. This is exactly the kind of embarrassment ESL learners fear when they open their mouths and try to use words they just learned. Learning a new word in English can make you soar, or drop you in quicksand.

Writing Centers as Language Centers

Ironically, conundrums like the difference between *flight* and *flighty* or *weight* and *weighty* are one reason why ESL students visit writing centers in the first place. They hope to find a place where they can interact with native speakers and discuss those aspects of the language that puzzle them. Tutors are usually happy to have the interaction but not very fluent when it comes to discussing linguistic puzzles: "That's just the way we say it." Heavy sigh. Why can't we explain our language to ESL students in ways that make sense?

Some tutors may believe English is made up of random rules and no real explanation is possible. Or perhaps they are not familiar enough with linguistic concepts to be able to answer ESL students' questions. Either way, the truth is that most of what might appear to be random in the way language works can be explained, though not always simply. Like all languages, English is a product of complex rules, intricate patterns, diverse cultures, and a lot of history. This means that the simple grammar rules we may have learned in junior high don't even begin to tell the story of how English is really put together. Tutors who can begin to understand the reasons for why English works the way it does will begin to appreciate the labyrinthine set of dos and don'ts their ESL writers have to navigate every day, and they will make some fascinating discoveries about the elegantly simple patterns that lie deep beneath the labyrinth, as linguists have done with discoveries about universal grammar; they will not only see how much more interesting language really is than when their junior high grammar teachers drilled it into them, but they will be able to provide more helpful answers to their nonnative-speaking tutees.

Let's return for a moment to the puzzle we encountered at the beginning of this chapter over the way certain adjectives seem to have special requirements for where they can be used. We saw that unlike most adjectives, some, like the word *previous*, work only with nouns and never with verbs; they are known as nonpredicable adjectives. Others are just the opposite, like *awash*, and prefer the company of verbs over nouns; they are predicable adjectives. Let's assume that we could explain this to our ESL students when the need arises. So far, so good. But there is more, and this is an example of why it is beneficial for tutors to learn more than the minimum about the ways their language works. The difference between predicable and nonpredicable adjectives is complicated by the fact that even though some adjectives work in both positions (recall *flimsy jacket* and *the jacket is flimsy*), they only make sense based on the noun they are paired with. Take the adjective *nuclear*, for instance. A *nuclear bomb* is a bomb that is nuclear, but a *nuclear scientist* is not a scientist that is nuclear. Similarly, *a nervous writer* is a writer who is nervous, but *a nervous habit* is not a habit that is nervous. And as if the situation were not confusing enough, sometimes an adjective-noun combination results in ambiguity so that one interpretation is as plausible as the other: Does *dramatic criticism* refer to criticism of drama or to criticism that is dramatic?[8] This can be a frustrating thing for nonnative speakers to deal with, and tutors need to be patient when students struggle with it. There is no fairy dust to sprinkle on these adjective-noun combinations that will unlock the logic behind them, but there are ways to test whether an adjective is predicable or nonpredicable, and this can help nonnative speakers make some sense of the situation. Space does not permit the full details of this test, but you can read about them in many linguistics texts, such as George Miller's *The Science of Words*. Until then, here is a hint: nonpredicable adjectives are not pure adjectives, like *flimsy*, but are variations of nouns: *previous, nuclear, nervous,* and *dramatic* are take-offs on the nouns *preview, nucleus, nerve,* and *drama.*

Sometimes we tend to overlook the mistakes we make as native speakers and to exaggerate the errors of nonnative speakers. It's good to remember that English lays down enough challenges for all of us. One of the most interesting is the plural form of words called headless compounds. They are puzzling because they make us stop and think why we treat them the way we do. Words like *Walkman, low-life,* and *flatfoot* form their plurals by simply adding *s* (Walkman*s*, low-life*s*, and flatfoot*s*), and this is contrary to the way we would pluralize them if they were simply *man, life,* and *foot*. What's going on here? And how do we explain it to ESL students? It's a fascinating puzzle, and one that no one explains better than linguist Steven Pinker.[9] Could it be that *Walkmans, low-lifes,* and *flatfoots* are just exceptions? The short answer is that our brains do not think of *Walkmans, low-lifes,* and *flatfoots* as types of men, lives, and feet. If they did, we would treat them like the irregular nouns they are and pluralize them accordingly as Walkmen, low-lives, and flatfeet. Instead, our brains store these words according to what they refer to—electronic devices, undesirable people, and detectives. When we ask our brains to pluralize these words, they tells us to follow the main rule for making plurals and just add *s*. In other words, our linguistic brains won't be fooled by mixing up these look-alikes with the real thing. So, the brain regularizes them, and will continue to do the same with any other screwball compound. Interested in buying a new pair of shoeloafs? They'd look good with your derby-dices. Alas, English shows it can be regular and predictable when you least expect it.

English from a Linguistic Perspective

Admittedly, figuring out how English works is something you can not just squeeze in between tutoring sessions. So what is a tutor to do when he find himself speechless over some aspect of English that cries out for explanation? Acknowledge the truth and admit you don't know. Then, make it a point to find the answer and become a student of the language. Until we try to understand the patterns that shape the way our language works, we know the language in only a very narrow and limited way. There is no simple or easy strategy to overcome these limitations when they arise in tutoring sessions. The only way to overcome them is to study English from a linguistic perspective by observing, reading, asking questions, and pursuing answers wherever you can find them. Doing so not only makes for some fascinating discoveries; it will also bring about more interesting and helpful interactions with the students we tutor.

Those of us who are native speakers of English may wonder why it is important to learn, say, the linguistic theory that lies behind a language we learned as children. As evidence, we could point to the fact that even many composition teachers in the United States downplay the importance of learning grammar, believing that all of the grammatical knowledge students need for writing will emerge naturally. If this is true, tutors may wonder, then what is the point of tutors learning about the structure of English? The answer is that it helps you to see why you know what you know about English, and it makes you a more informed and helpful tutor for people who don't know English but want to learn it. To appreciate these facts, consider the discoveries of the most important linguist of our time, Noam Chomsky, who proved that grammatical knowledge is bestowed upon every human being as a birthright.[10] He observed that native speakers possess insights into their language that even the most advanced linguistic theories strain to describe. For example, native speakers recognize that a sentence like *They are eating apples* can have two entirely different meanings because they know intuitively that *eating* functions as a verb in one interpretation and as a modifier of the noun *apples* in the other. Native English speakers know this even though they may never have studied grammar or learned the terms *verb*, *modifier*, or *noun*. How long does it take you to recognize the two different meanings in each of the following sentences?

Billy grew a foot last year.

Visiting relatives can be a nuisance.

They loaded the cart in the parking lot.

I love her dancing.

And an old favorite of linguists (cover your ears)—

It takes two mice to screw in a light bulb.

It's hard not to be amused by sentences like these because each one is perfectly grammatical and yet conveys two distinctly different meanings. We can see that they are well-formed and can imagine contexts where they would make sense (for example: With the help of advanced cloning techniques, Billy grew a foot last year, reversing a birth defect that had left him with only one appendage). We recognize the two meanings because we possess knowledge about parts of speech, word meanings, and how words go together that enables us to decode the dual meanings almost effortlessly. Computers can decode them too, of course, but not before they are programmed with the equivalent of a library full of dictionaries and linguistic algorithms. As native speakers, we also know instantly when a phrase or sentence written by a nonnative speaker is not right or not English-sounding. The point of these examples is to show that even though as native speakers we possess an instinct for using our language, we don't usually have much insight into the framework of this knowledge, and we definitely don't have the vocabulary to talk about the knowledge until we begin to study it—by taking some linguistics classes, reading books that delve into it[11] (see the Works Cited at the end of this chapter and other chapters), and becoming more observant of the language patterns that surround us all. Once we do, we will find that discovering this knowledge and learning how to discuss it can be as rewarding for us as for those we teach and tutor.

Notes

1. Two useful books on English as a global phenomenon are Kachru, Strevens, and Ayers (1992) and Crystal (1998).
2. Andersson, 50.
3. Andersson, 50–51.
4. Miller, 135.
5. McCrum, Cran, and MacNeil (1992).
6. McCrum, 29.
7. There are many good, free websites to help ESL students with prepositions, articles, and other troublesome parts of English. One is *http://cctc2.commnet.edu/grammar/prepositions.*
8. Miller, 195.
9. Pinker, 141–45.
10. Pinker.
11. Tutors who are interested in the science and psychology of language, including the ideas of Noam Chomsky, will find these two books, as well as Pinker (1994), accessible and interesting: Bialystok and Hakuta (1994) and Jackendoff (1994).

Works Cited

Andersson, Lars-Gunnar. 1998. "Some Languages Are Harder Than Others." In *Language Myths*, edited by Laurie Lauer and Peter Trudgill, 50–57. New York: Penguin.

Bialystok, Ellen, and Kenji Hakuta. 1994. *In Other Words: The Science and Psychology of Second Language Acquisition*. New York: Basic Books.

Crystal, David. 1998. *English as a Global Language*. New York: Cambridge University Press.

Jackendoff, Ray. 1994. *Patterns in the Mind*. New York: Basic Books.

Kachru, Braj, Peter Strevens, and Lauren K. Ayers, eds. 1992. *The Other Tongue*. Urbana, IL: University of Illinois Press.

McCrum, Robert, William Cran, and Robert MacNeil. 1992. *The Story of English*. Rev. ed. New York: Penguin.

Miller, George A. 1996. *The Science of Words*. New York: W. H. Freeman.

Pinker, Steven. 1994. *The Language Instinct*. New York: William Morrow.

15

ESL Students Share Their Writing Center Experiences

Shanti Bruce

Ben Rafoth and I decided that it was important to include a last chapter that returned the focus of the collection from theories of culture and linguistic concerns to the individual student because after all, that is what our work and this publication are ultimately about. Toward that end, this chapter is devoted to sharing excerpts from several conversations I had with second language writers attending universities across the northeastern United States. Before writing this chapter, I asked each of them to spend some time talking with me about their experiences learning to write in English and using the writing center. With their permission, I taped our conversations and preserved much of their speech patterns in the transcription process. Adding their perspective reminds us that each English as a second language (ESL) student we encounter is an individual. In this chapter, we go beyond just hearing their voices and their personal experiences to reflecting on what we can learn from each one: how they impact our understanding of culture and how tutors may conduct themselves more effectively during writing conferences. We explore times when tutor feedback sheets may not tell the whole story, when privacy becomes an issue, when a student's cultural background causes tutors to be judged on age instead of skill, what happens when students don't understand the mission of the writing center, and more.

The topics emerged directly from the conversations and relate to the specific information and suggestions offered in previous chapters. For example, we will meet Sami, Jung-jun, and Helene, who all express their insecurities about visiting the writing center for fear of being seen as weak students. Jung-jun also questions tutors' capabilities if they do not meet her culturally based criteria for writing instructors: they must have extensive experience and be older than she is. These issues of privacy and elder-as-teacher are culturally based and influence the tutoring session, frequently without the tutor's knowledge. Nancy Hayward discusses these and several other cultural issues in Chapter 1. Jung-jun's comments about how important her first impression of a tutor is to the success of the session directly relates to suggestions in Chapter 3 about making a good start. And when Zahara expresses how helpful it is to have her paper read aloud by a tutor, we can look to Paul Matsuda and Michelle Cox's advice in Chapter 4 about how to pick the right approach to reading a student's paper.

I encourage directors and tutors to experience their writing center environments through the eyes of their second language students. For me, talking with ESL students directly about their needs and experiences made my own study of abstract theories and pedagogical practices come alive. The students you will meet could have easily sat in any one of our centers asking for help, and they reveal some of what we are and are not accomplishing during conferences. I hope that this chapter will prompt even more discussions among tutors about the experiences of second language writers when working with native English-speaking tutors in the writing center.

Sami

I waited for Sami near the coffee bar in the library. It was a warm Saturday afternoon, and I looked forward to meeting him since our only correspondence had been through e-mail. I came early and sat at a table facing the entrance. We spotted each other at the same time. I stood and smiled as Sami walked toward me. He was a major presence—tall with a full beard. His eyes were bright, and as we shook hands, he offered a kind smile.

At the beginning of our conversation, Sami told me that he was a student from Saudi Arabia and that he had started at the university in a bridge program designed to help students prepare for credit bearing classes. He also said that I should know before we began that he didn't use the writing center. I was stunned. I knew I had clearly explained the topic of the project through our correspondence, and he had never let on that he wasn't a candidate. Unsure of where to go from there, I asked him why he had agreed to meet with me. He said that he didn't want to say "no" when I asked for his participation. I was stunned again at his desire to help me with this project despite the fact that he didn't think he had much to contribute.

As it turned out, my meeting with Sami added a great deal. He mentioned that he had in fact been to the writing center a couple of times but that he quit going. I asked him to tell me about that, and he explained the reasons he stopped going. He said that the tutors were not capable and that he had not received the kind of help he needed. I wasn't completely convinced by his reasons for not using the writing center because he was the only Middle-Eastern male student on campus to agree to meet with me. I had asked several, and while they were all friendly, they consistently said that they had no experience with the writing center. Eventually, Sami revealed the real reason he avoided the writing center, and it had nothing to do with the tutors' skills. His was an issue of privacy and of being seen as weak by others.

By examining the cultural issues of privacy and pride, we learn firsthand how cultural influences are sometimes responsible for students' dissatisfaction with writing center experiences. This also proves to be an example of a time when tutor feedback sheets might not have told the whole story. Sami would most likely have written down the same reasons for his dissatisfaction that he initially shared with me. It took him a long time to become comfortable enough to share the truth during our conversation, and I believe those feelings would never have made it onto a tutor feedback sheet.

He began:

> Whenever I start a writing assignment, I have this difficulty of arranging my ideas, putting my main topic, supporting what I wanted to say. Really, I didn't have that ability to write a good writing, so I went to the writing center asking some people who work there to help me. I made it once or twice, but I didn't find it helpful because what they were doing is just looking for the grammar stuff and the grammatical mistakes and things on the surface. While I didn't want that, what I wanted was somebody who tells me about the ideas, how to explore my ideas, how to put my ideas, how to write the theme of the topic or the piece of writing that I wanted to write and how should I support my theme or my main topic.

Sami articulated his dissatisfaction with the writing center staff's ability to help him with global writing concerns. Many writing center response forms make it easy to mark these types of concerns, and he would have likely been comfortable mentioning them to a professor or writing center director. He went on to call into question the competency of the tutors based on their age and experience.

> Many of these people who work at the writing center do not know how to work with the ESL students, so I thought that they were not able to help me the way I want. I did not ask them directly to go in-depth, but from the one or the two times that I went, I felt that they just looked at the surface things, so I decided not to go there anymore and try to look for someone who is in a higher education level. I'm assuming that he or she will be interested in working with ESL students.

Sami insisted that the writing center was to blame for his decision to stop going, but because I found Middle-Eastern male students' avoidance of the writing center so noticeably different from the African and Asian student populations, I asked one more question to try to get to the bottom of this apparent cultural difference. I asked Sami if he would go back to the writing center if a graduate student who had experience working with ESL students met with him and addressed all of his global writing issues in the ways that he had described to me. Forty minutes into our conversation, Sami finally revealed the truth.

> OK, I didn't want to go to that place where everybody can see me sitting and talking about the papers. I wanted to stay in private with the person whom I feel comfortable with and have the discussion and the working privately. That is the reason I preferred not to continue going to the writing center. Maybe

from the cultural perspective, I don't want so many people to see me as the one that is in this program and whose ability in writing is weak. From the couple of classes I went to, I found myself not qualified enough to write the way that the professors want me to write. For a simple reason is that I haven't been taught in a way that I should be writing because back home they do not focus attention to enhancing the writing ability of us as ESL learners. They focus on the speaking, the listening to some extent, the reading, but I believe my weakness is in writing. The moment I noticed that, I said, "OK, I need to work on this weakness, but I want to make it as private as possible. I don't want the others to know about my weakness."

Sami looked away from me while he admitted these things, and I thanked him for his honesty. Clearly, he would never have written these comments on a feedback sheet. I could not have predicted that Sami would have such extensive writing problems. He had an impressive vocabulary and spoke clearly and confidently, but as Paul Matsuda and Michelle Cox explain in Chapter 4, quoting Alister Cumming, "the relationship between language proficiency and writing proficiency is not simple; the ability to speak English does not necessarily correspond directly with the quality of texts [ESL students] produce." As we were leaving the library, he continued to tell me that Middle-Eastern men generally do not want to be seen as needing help, and he asked me again to make sure to use his pseudonym.

Sami's story illustrates a writing center dilemma common among native and nonnative-English-speaking students. They need the help the writing center offers, but they are embarrassed to admit it.

In this case, cultural issues, not the competency of the tutors, were responsible for keeping a certain student population away from the writing center. In Chapter 13, Gerd Bräuer names "not coming to the writing center at all" as one of the common problems among ESL writers. Sami's background made it impossible for him to feel comfortable getting help in a public area such as the writing center. For Sami, the writing center setting compromised his need for privacy when getting help and created the opportunity for shame should he be perceived as weak by others. Nancy Hayward, Chapter 1, explores the fear of appearing weak, and in her section on intercultural communication, she discusses beliefs about accepting or demanding help. Uncomfortable with the idea of needing help in the first place, Sami did not want to be seen publicly accepting it. Privacy issues such as these can be addressed by providing meeting spaces that are private or semiprivate, but if resources don't permit, at least directors and tutors will know that sometimes there are reasons, beyond what is written on the feedback sheet, for why some students are not happy with their writing center experiences.

Jung-jun

When I heard that Jung-jun used the writing center regularly, I approached her about this project, and she agreed to meet with me on a Friday afternoon. We chatted casually about the weather and her program of study as we climbed the stairs to the library study room I had reserved. I learned that she had spent her summer auditing classes and that she took her studies very seriously.

I began by asking Jung-jun how she had heard about the writing center, and she carried the conversation by recounting experience after experience and offering many strong opinions. She was particularly adamant about the qualities she expected from writing tutors. She insisted that a qualified tutor would be older than she was, have extensive writing and tutoring experience, and be a native speaker of English. While Jung-jun began talking with bold confidence, it wasn't long before she softened and shared more personal experiences and feelings. She admitted to some of the same insecurities Sami had expressed, including the fear of being seen as incapable or unprepared for instruction in a U.S. university, and she described experiences that had left her confused and uneasy. Many topics emerged while talking with Jung-jun, and from these we learn about cultural expectations, insecurities, and communication challenges.

Jung-jun began:

> I came here as a second language learner from Korea. My teacher recommended, "You can go to writing center," but I had no idea what is that. Maybe probably they help in writing, but yeah, wow, there is a writing center! In my country, no writing center.

In Chapter 13, Gerd Bräuer points out that many second language students do not know about or understand the writing center. He urges writing center directors to "advertise broadly on campus not only the existence, but also the kind of work a writing center is doing." For example, ESL students often don't realize that writing centers generally aim to go beyond surface issues to talking about the content of a paper at any stage during the writing process.

Jung-jun had a lot to say about the age, experience, and nationality of the tutors.

> Sometimes I feel tutor is pretty young. When they are younger than me, I don't trust them. Teacher has to be older; then I can trust them. I would rather not an undergraduate student help me. I would like for graduate student and an American, so I feel that he knows something. I wonder if they had to be tested before becoming a tutor. I doubt them, but maybe they are good students, right? Probably good writers, right? I want to see what is their experience. What, do they publish writing? Is usually a tutor from English department? Sometimes I am not sure they are really qualified. I've never had an international student as my tutor. I saw an international student tutor, but I didn't get help from her because I wonder how well she really writes? I doubt she writes well.

From these statements, we learn that some students have very specific beliefs about who they think is capable of being a good tutor. Though it may seem unfair that Jung-jun was unwilling to give an international student tutor a chance and would have clearly been unhappy if she had to meet with a younger, undergraduate tutor, her beliefs are strong and come from years of cultural influences. In her section on "Psychological and Social Aspects," Hayward explains that "some ESL students may distrust younger tutors, feeling they do not have the experience and authority of older, more experienced tutors" (Chapter 1). Bräuer names this "specific understanding of the role of the tutor as . . . teacher" among the common problems ESL writers have with the writing center. He says that these students often "try to manipulate the tutor to fit their expectations" (Chapter 13). Students like Jung-jun usually do not enter each new tutoring situation with an open mind but with longstanding culturally specific expectations. In Chapter 1, Hayward explains how "the culture from which we come has much to do with our assumptions of the way things 'ought to be.'" While making the tutors' qualifications public might alleviate some students' concerns, we should learn from this that students might not always be judging their tutors solely on their professionalism and ability to communicate and aid in the writing process.

Similar to Sami, Jung-jun expressed her insecurities about being perceived as needing help when she told me about a time when her writing center tutor turned out to be one of her classmates.

> One day, tutor was my classmate, so I don't want to show my paper to him. It was kind of like, awkward. It was weird. This was an older, American student, but still I don't feel comfortable. I don't feel confident because I need help. He doesn't have to come to writing center because he can do his without help. So I feel . . . I shrink. I know he was capable of helping, but I don't want because maybe he look at me and think, "You're here in the [United States], and you still need a writing helper?"

I saw the embarrassment on her face as she told me about this experience. She drew clenched fists tightly into her chest and her voice got low when she said, "I shrink." I am reminded of Hayward's explanations in Chapter 1 about how low self-confidence and beliefs about accepting help affect intercultural communication. Students like Jung-jun may feel more comfortable if they have a better understanding of who uses the writing center. Most writing centers are no longer considered primarily places of remediation. In fact, successful students visit the writing center everyday because they know the value of having a second reader. They understand how a fresh pair of eyes can spot a misstep in a paper and how talking about ideas with another person can clarify meanings. Graduate students and tutors alike recognize the advantage of exchanging papers and receiving feedback, but not all students, especially international, realize the true mission of the writing center and who actually frequents it. Why ESL students may not understand the U.S. conception of a writing center is discussed further in Chapter 13.

Jung-jun continued our conversation by telling me about a recent experience that left her feeling troubled.

> Two weeks ago, I met a woman tutor, and she said, "Okay, what do you want me to do?" And I said, "Check grammar," but she said, "You know what?"

Sometimes people abuse tutors." She said that! I was surprised! She said, "People just bring a draft in and then ask a tutor to make the paper into final version, but it takes a lot of time." She thought that's abuse! I know what she said, but I try as much as I can.

Jung-jun got very animated as she told me about this encounter. She was especially concerned about the tutor's use of the word "abuse," which she considered inappropriate and harsh. According to Jung-jun, the tutor was accusing her of attempting to abuse both her and the situation. Jung-jun was caught off guard and became defensive and confused by the tutor's remarks.

If this situation happened as Jung-jun recounted it, would she have been justified in lodging a complaint with the director? In most writing centers, yes, because the tutor would have been considered at fault for assuming the worst and taking out her frustrations on a tutee. If the tutor felt that this was becoming a serious problem, perhaps she should have taken the time to explain to Jung-jun that the writing center's policy is not to edit student papers but to talk about global concerns, including content, organization, and clarification of meanings. First and second language writers often don't know how to ask for help with anything besides grammar, so this explanation would provide Jung-jun with more options. Then, if Jung-jun insisted she needed help with grammar, the tutor could have agreed to focus on one or two items during the session. Afterward, the tutor could have taken her concerns to the director. The director and tutor could then decide how to deal with situations like this in the future.

But what if Jung-jun misinterpreted the situation and the tutor's intentions? Cultural backgrounds could be at the root of this awkward situation, and the tutor might be very surprised to hear Jung-jun's rendering of the encounter. In her section on "Cultural Preferences for Interpersonal Communication," Hayward discusses directness and indirectness (Chapter 1). She explains that "The United States is a country where directness, *telling it like it is* or *laying it all out on the table*, is valued. Other cultures find this approach blunt and offensive. . . . When tutors work with international students . . . they should understand that one culture's openness is another's rudeness." Perhaps Jung-jun mistook this tutor's culturally ingrained openness for rudeness.

This led Jung-jun to comment on tutor personalities and professionalism.

It is really important, my first impression. If in the beginning I feel comfortable, then I can talk more. If the tutor doesn't smile or is not kind, then it's like *oooh*. I'm really affected by the tutor's personality or attitude. There was a tutor—he doesn't even focus on my writing. I wasn't really happy with him because he's watching people going back and forth, and getting the phone, and he say to me, "Okay, I'll be right back in five minute." He kept leaving and coming back.

Jung-jun's desire to work with a kind person is not unique to ESL writers. Personalities and attitudes invariably set the tone for all sessions and affect productivity. It is certainly not too much to ask of a tutor, or a tutee, to make an effort to be pleasant and focus on the work at hand. (See Chapter 3 for more on opening a session.) While Jung-jun describes this situation as one in which she felt the tutor did not make an effort to devote his complete attention to her needs during the conference, I wonder if the same tutor might be admired by a native speaker for his ability to multitask, a skill valued by employers in the United States. What if the center became busy and he was the only tutor there at that hour? Who would answer the phone or the questions of the other students passing by? In most situations, an effort should always be made to minimize distractions during a writing conference, but should a tutor find herself in this situation, talking about the circumstances could prevent the feelings of neglect that Jung-jun experienced.

Zahara

Zahara showed up at the local coffee shop in a khaki suit with exquisite jewelry and purple lipstick. I noticed right away how striking she was. She told me that she was a professional woman as well as a wife and mother of two. She looked at her watch a couple of times indicating that she was eager to get down to business, so I began our conversation by asking her to tell me a little bit about herself.

> I am originally from Uganda, West Africa. My husband is now a professor here in the [United States], so I'm taking some courses on and off. My mother language is like Ugandan, but when you start school, you have to learn English because all of the textbooks are in English. Uganda is a British colony, so English is official language. Still though, I find it hard because American English is different from British English.

I then asked her how she learned about the writing center and how she felt about its services. Her responses were positive for many writing center practices. First, she praised the campus for having a place where students could get help with their writing. Then, she talked about how helpful it is to discuss her writing with another person and how she benefited from having her paper read aloud by a tutor. Without knowing the technical term, Zahara commented on the facilitative approach the tutors employed and how she grew more competent as a writer by learning to find the answers for herself. Her statements reflected writing center theory being put into practice, and she showed that these practices work for her and are appreciated.

> When I was taking English 101, our professor said, "You can go to writing lab if you feel like you need help when we're writing papers." I don't know about other people, but for me, I want a chance for someone to read my paper before I hand it to the professor. I mean sometime you may write a paper and don't have anyone to help you, so it was good that the writing lab was there and they can help you where your weakness is. So I used it, and it was helpful.

Zahara continued by talking about the way the tutors read her text out loud and how beneficial she found this practice.

> I had good experiences with them. Sometimes I'll write the paper and every-thing sounds good, but when they read it, they'll catch some things like organization and grammar that I didn't catch. When you read your paper, some-times you don't see the mistakes and the tutor does. It was very helpful. I took each assignment there two times. I prefer for the tutor to read it out loud, so you can just listen and catch your own mistakes. When you hear someone else reading it, you find the mistake and you correct it. It's like it is their paper.

For Zahara, this provides an opportunity to see her paper through someone else's eyes. In Chapter 4, Matsuda and Cox explain that while it often helps native speakers to read their drafts aloud, "It may be more helpful for the ESL writer to hear the tutor read the paper out loud—to note when the reader stumbles, pauses, fills in missing articles and modifiers, or reads smoothly." In fact, "for many ESL writers, reading their paper out loud may shift their attention to the pronunciation of the English language—a proficiency separate from writing in English."

Next, Zahara commented specifically on the facilitative techniques the tutors used to help her learn to correct her own mistakes.

> When I went there, they would help with grammar, organization. And some-times I'm not so good with spelling. They would say, "Here, maybe you mis-spelled this." You write on your paper because they like for you to be handling it. You sit next to each other and do it together. I would put a note on it with a red pen, so when I go home I can use a dictionary, and that helps me to learn more because I am correcting my own mistakes and seeing what I did wrong. I always remembered what to change because when they were teaching me, I made sure to write everything I needed to correct.

Here Zahara identifies her need for error correction, something writing centers typically shy away from. In Chapter 8, Cynthia Linville says that sometimes, attending to errors is just what the student needs. In fact, recent writing center research suggests "lifting the ban against proofreading." Linville explains that "When a student can learn what her most frequent errors are, and learn to rec-ognize and correct her own mistakes, then she will be a proficient self-editor." Luckily for Zahara, she met with tutors who were willing to work with her on error correction in a way that would ultimately help her to help herself.

Zahara also mentions that she "always remembered what to change because . . . [she] made sure to write everything" down as they went along. This is a good strategy for tutees to use during conferences; however, some ESL writers may not have the writing proficiency needed to take notes during con-ferences. In Chapter 7, Jennifer Staben and Kathryn Dempsey Nordhaus sug-gest that "one of the simplest things you can do for students is to serve as a scribe." Assisting students in recording the topics covered and suggestions made during the conference will go a long way toward the success of the meeting and the goal of helping writers to become proficient self-editors.

Zahara ended our conversation with even more praise for the center and the role it played in her success as a student.

> They have a comment sheet there where you grade the tutor and write how it went. Everybody got high grades from me. I got an A in my class, and I think that if I didn't go there I wouldn't have gotten an A. I recommend it to other people because I always felt comfortable there. They have different tutors there, but everybody I met, male/female, they all knew what they were doing. I never asked if they were graduate or undergraduate students. It didn't matter because they gave me what I wanted.

Every tutor hopes tutees will leave their conferences feeling as satisfied as Zahara was. While results so consistent are impossible, it is inspiring to hear positive accounts from pleased students. Besides sharing stories like this with tutors during staff meetings, Bräuer encourages centers to "Publicize outstanding results of student writing that profited from the interaction with the writing center . . . to demonstrate that *everyone* can improve as a writer" (Chapter 13).

Jane and Yoshi

An ESL professor introduced me to Hui Ping, a Taiwanese student, and Yoshi, a Japanese student, between classes one day. Hui Ping immediately asked me to call her Jane because that was the "American name" her teacher in Taiwan had given her. I asked her if she liked being called Jane. She paused for a moment, and then looked up at me and said, "No, we didn't like the names, but she just gave them to us. But you call me Jane." I could see that she was used to a rigid education system, but that she had definite opinions of her own. I agreed to call her Jane and thought briefly about how accustomed she was to not questioning authority and how that might affect the tutor/tutee relationship.

I followed Jane and Yoshi into an empty classroom and began to talk with them about how they learned about the writing center. Jane told me that one of her professors had told her class about it, and Yoshi said,

> I heard about the writing center from my friend. He was from Japan too and told me that there is a kind of place where native tutors are kindly helping students with their writing assignments. We can go there as much as we want for free, so I go there almost all the time I have writing assignments, plus whenever I need to make error-free English sentences.

Yoshi mentioned visiting the center anytime he "need[s] to make error-free English sentences," which includes filling out school forms and job applications, writing resumes, letters, e-mails, and anything else requiring clear writing in English. Yoshi likes using the campus writing center to fulfill all of these needs, but whether these services are really the job of the writing center is debatable. Paula Gillespie explores this conundrum in Chapter 11, remarking that "This is a question we ask often in writing center work, but international students are by no means the only ones who make us wonder about the boundaries of our tutoring jobs." She discusses many questionable uses of the writing center, and concludes by saying that these decisions will have to be made by directors on an individual basis and will "surely depend on how busy your center is, on the demand for writing help."

After discussing these issues with Yoshi, the conversation turned to Jane. She agreed that writing center conferences were helpful, but said she often felt frustrated when she tried to go back and actually make the changes in her paper after the conference.

> Sometimes when I went back and tried to correct what the tutor helped me with, I find that I am confused. Did she say to write like this or that? Sometimes, we don't go back to check it again, so it will be mixed up. If we can do things like that, go over it the first time and the second time we read it the correct way, it will be more organized, more helpful. I know that they don't have so much time to go over the second time, but I get confused when we don't.

Unlike Zahara, Jane did not take efficient notes during the conference and ended up forgetting much of what was discussed. Staben and Nordhaus remind us that "the spoken word can be extremely powerful, but when placed on a page, writers tend to think of it as permanent" (Chapter 7). Jane is one student who would benefit from having a tutor serve as scribe. "Harness[ing] the power of paper to work for the student's benefit" is explained in detail in Chapter 7.

Recalling what Hayward explains in Chapter 1 as the Japanese tendency to give vocal indications they are listening much more than Americans, Yoshi stayed very much in the conversation by nodding and agreeing while Jane was talking. When I tried to turn the conversation back to him, he wasn't able to give me any real specifics about his experiences. He simply stated that he didn't have any complaints, and that "the tutors are always very hard-working and willing to help." I hope that this is true, but I wonder if Yoshi held back a little because of his desire to be polite. Did Yoshi see me as an advocate of the writing center? Did he not want to offend me by showing any dissatisfaction with his experiences? Was I second-guessing too much?

Jane offered to say more about her experiences. She commented on her struggles mastering U.S. forms of language. She talked about trying to translate her ideas from Chinese into English and her fear of losing meaning in translation due to incorrect forms and phrasing.

> I go there because I want to make sure that my writing is correct. When I write a paper, I translate my idea from my language to English. My first language is Chinese, so for example, "Tomorrow I'm going to the supermarket." I think it in Chinese, and I try to translate the idea into English, but you know with translation there will be something happen, like maybe the American people

don't say the sentence like this, but actually the grammar is correct, but people don't say things like this. So, I want to make sure.

Even if the ESL writer you are working with has had a great deal of experience writing in English, she may still worry that her form gets in the way of communication. In Chapter 7, Staben and Nordhaus encourage tutors to ask questions and interact with a tutee's text so that the writer will see how a reader views his work. This is what Jane is looking for when she visits the writing center.

Jane's translation conflict between Chinese and English demonstrates the difficulty of translating an idea from one language to another. Her strategy of thinking in Chinese and translating into English is having limited success because there are concepts, even words, that defy one-to-one translations. By showing her writing to a tutor, Jane can make sure that translation has not skewed her intended meanings.

Helene

Because of distance, I had to settle for e-mail correspondence with Helene. As with everyone else, I asked her to tell me about her experiences working with native English-speaking tutors at the writing center. Eager to share her stories with me, Helene responded to my inquiry promptly, including comments on the skills she needed to improve and her insecurities about visiting the writing center.

> My English writing skills were rather poor. My thoughts were disorganized and unconnected. My grammar was at times unbearable, as I switched tenses and wrote according to a German grammar scheme. In addition, I used many Genglish (German/English) words that aren't usually used or not in the particular content that I was using them. I went to the writing center with the determination to improve upon those weaknesses.

Helene found herself following the rhetorical strategies of her first language, German, while writing in English, and knew that it was interfering with the meanings she was trying to convey. Like Jane, Helene needed the eyes and ears of native-speaking tutors to help her learn to control the form of her writing. Hayward explains contrastive rhetoric as "the ways that cultures differ in their expectations about rhetorical patterns or logical organization of a text" (Chapter 1). Staben and Nordhaus also cover ESL students' insecurities about form in Chapter 7.

Similar to Sami and Jung-jun, Helene also expressed insecurities about going to the writing center. At first, she thought it would mark her as a weak student and felt self-conscious about admitting her problems with writing.

> At first, I was a little bit embarrassed to go to the center, since I viewed it as being there for especially weak students, and I definitely wasn't going to count myself among those. However, I started to feel more comfortable accepting their services when I realized that writing is like any other subject

and that not being able to express one's views clearly through writing is nothing to be ashamed of. It's not a disease. It takes work to learn to write, and that
is what the writing center is there for.

Because of the writing center, both Helene's writing and her self-esteem
improved. She learned that problems with writing are simply problems with
writing. They are not an indication of intelligence or a determiner of potential.

Sami, Jung-jun, Zahara, Jane, Yoshi, and Helene provided us with firsthand
accounts of their writing center experiences. What we learn from them is now
up to us. Take these stories and talk about them. Interact with them, learn from
them, and build on them. Whether we are faced with the challenge of calming
feelings of insecurity, recognizing and understanding cultural divides, or simply editing line by line, our jobs are at once arduous and rewarding. But the
incentive to keep working and to keep learning lies in the possibility that each
new day will bring one more student closer to understanding and enjoying the
process of learning to write in English.

Glossary

English   A dominant or official language in more than sixty countries, with numerous **varieties**. English is the primary language in the United States, United Kingdom, Ireland, Canada, Australia, and New Zealand, with the United States having the greatest number of native speakers. Many people also learn English as their native tongue in multilingual countries such as India, Liberia, and Jamaica.

behaviorism   As applied to language, behaviorism is the theoretical view that language learning occurs through habit formation. Learners mimic the language they hear, and when they receive positive feedback, that language becomes a habit. Critics believe it does not explain how a child can acquire something as complex as a language with so little input and feedback. Compare **innatism**.

bilingual   The ability to speak two languages almost equally well.

collocations   Words that tend to be associated with each other. Some words that collocate well with *wedding*, for example, are *white, cake, ring, shotgun*, and *vows*. Collocates are important in ESL because they help to explain why a learner's language can be grammatically correct and have clear meaning, yet the utterance seems strange. For example, in North America, *I am going to clean my teeth* is grammatically correct and comprehensible, but *teeth* collocates so well with brush that it seems awkward. Collocations often interfere in nativelike production as learners substitute the collocations from their own language into English grammar. Korean ESL learners, for example, may say, *I am going to go eye-shopping* in place of *window-shopping*.

Contrastive Rhetoric   An area of research based on differences across cultures and used to help ESL learners understand English rhetorics by comparing them with the rhetorics of other cultures.

EFL   English as a foreign language. Refers to English taught and learned in a country where it is not the primary language, for example, Japan.

ELL   English language learner. A more general term that avoids distinguishing between English as a second, third, or fourth (etc.) language.

ESL   English as a second language. *ESL* is used when English is a speaker's second, third, or fourth (etc.) language, within a country where English is the primary language.

error   An incorrect usage that occurs when learners don't know the correct form; errors relate to a failure in competence, having the wrong knowledge or lack of knowledge. Compare **mistake**.

fluent   The ability to speak or write easily and smoothly.

fossilization   Occurs when an **error** becomes a habit of speech, and the learner's language becomes automatic before it is nativelike.

Generation 1.5   A label used to refer to students between first-generation immigrants (foreign-born and foreign-educated) and second-generation immigrants (children of immigrants who are U.S.–born and –educated, and whose dominant language is English). These students come to the United States as children or adolescents. They possess some characteristics of their parents' culture and some of U.S. culture.

innatism   As applied to language, this is the theoretical view that children are born with knowledge of the structures of language. It is because of this innate knowledge that children can learn a complex language with relatively little input. Innatism can be contrasted with interactionism, a theory where meaningful interaction along with innate knowledge combine to make language acquisition possible. Compare **behaviorism**.

interlanguage   A stage in which language learners acquire forms of language that are in between their first language and their target language. For example, they incorrectly apply rules of their native language to their target language, or they have not completely learned the extent or limitations of a rule, and so they misapply it systematically or **overgeneralize**. It may seem correct in the mind of the language learner, and it may be a part of a natural learning process where rules become more refined as more input is received.

L1   An abbreviation for first language, native language, and mother tongue.

L2   An abbreviation for second language, **target language**, and the language learned after the first language is acquired.

language acquisition   The process by which children learn their native language, usually in the home. They can achieve full competence in speaking without any formal instruction.

language learning   The process by which we learn a language through formal instruction. Adults taking English classes are *learning* the language, not *acquiring* it. The distinction sometimes becomes blurred, as in the case of children learning a second language at school, or an adult picking up a language by living in the country but not taking language classes.

mistake   An incorrect usage that occurs when language learners know the correct form but, for whatever reason, don't use it; mistakes relate to a failure in performance, for example, a slip of the tongue or typos. Compare **error**.

NES   Native English speaker. Anyone for whom English is their first language, usually learned in the home.

NNES   Nonnative English speaker. Anyone for whom English is a second, third, or fourth (etc.) language.

NS   Native speaker.

NNS   Nonnative speaker.

native language   The language a person learns growing up, usually at home. Compare **L1**.

overgeneralization   Application of a language rule beyond its range. For example, students learn that superlative forms of adjectives can be made with -*est*, such as *nicest, quickest*, and so on. If they start to produce incorrect superlatives like *goodest, comfortablest,* and *expensivest*, they are overgeneralizing.

primary language   The first or native or dominant language spoken by an individual.

reformulation   A process in language learning that involves the revision of an incorrect statement. For example, changing green*room* effect to green*house* effect.

SLA   Second language acquisition. A term for the field of study that has to do with learning a second, third, and fourth (etc.) language.

target language   The language one is trying to learn or use (besides the L1).

TEFL   Teaching English as a foreign language. See **EFL**.

TESL   Teaching English as a second language. See **ESL**.

TESOL   Teaching English to Speakers of Other Languages. Refers to both the field of study and the professional association.

variety   A term used by linguists often instead of *dialect, argot, jargon, slang,* and so on. For example, in the United States, Southern dialect, Black English Vernacular, and Standard American English are all *varieties* of English.

Contributors

Kurt Bouman teaches writing and directs the writing center at Indiana University of Pennsylvania's (IUP) Punxsutawney campus. He is a PhD candidate in Composition and TESOL at IUP; his current research focuses on plagiarism and authorship. He has discovered that if Punxsutawney Phil visits your writing center and his shadow falls across your draft, you'll need to write six more revisions.

Gerd Bräuer is Associate Professor of German Studies at Emory University. He was DAAD Professor at the University of Education Freiburg (Germany) from 2001–2003. Most recent book publication include *Pedagogy of Language Learning in Higher Education* (Ablex, 2001), *Body and Language: Intercultural Learning Through Drama* (Greenwood, 2002), and *Teaching Academic Writing in Higher Education* (Kluwer, co-ed., 2003), *New Visions in Foreign and Second Language Education* (LARC Press, co-ed., 2004).

Shanti Bruce is a PhD candidate in Composition and TESOL at Indiana University of Pennsylvania, where she is a graduate assistant in the writing center and conducted the research that served as the springboard for *ESL Writers: A Guide for Writing Center Tutors.* She has taught composition courses at the University of North Alabama and is currently conducting research on the leadership practices of faculty who lead university writing programs.

Michelle Cox is a PhD student in Composition Studies at the University of New Hampshire. She teaches various composition and literature courses, and worked in and around the Robert J. Connors Writing Center for years. Her research interests include second language writing, writing across the curriculum, and professional writing.

Kevin Dvorak is a PhD candidate in Composition and TESOL at Indiana University of Pennsylvania, where he is also the assistant director of the writing center. Formerly, he was the writing center assistant director at Sonoma State University, where he began his quest to bring the act of creative writing into the writing center.

Paula Gillespie directs the writing center at Marquette University, where she also teaches a tutoring training course. She has served as president of the International Writing Centers Association since 2001. The second edition of her book, *The Allyn and Bacon Guide to Peer Tutoring*, co-authored with Neal Lerner, appeared in 2003.

Nancy Hayward teaches undergraduate and graduate classes in the English Department at Indiana University of Pennsylvania. Her research interests include popular linguistics, intercultural communication, discourse analysis, ESL theory and methods, composition, and language and gender. She has lived and taught in Egypt, Mexico, and Bulgaria.

Cynthia Linville teaches both mainstream and ESL composition courses at California State University, Sacramento. She is currently conducting research in error correction comparing native English speakers and ESL students, and in intercultural communication between American and international students. She conducted her graduate research in a university writing center.

Paul Kei Matsuda is Assistant Professor of English and Associate Director of Composition at the University of New Hampshire, where he teaches various writing courses as well as graduate courses in composition studies and applied linguistics. He has co-edited several books, including *Landmark Essays on ESL Writing* (Erlbaum, 2001) and *On Second Language Writing* (Erlbaum, 2001).

Amy Jo Minett is a PhD candidate in Composition and TESOL at Indiana University of Pennsylvania (IUP). She has taught and tutored ESL writing in Hungary, Romania, Serbia, and most recently, at IUP. A published poet, she has also launched and edited two creative writing journals for second language writers.

Kathryn Dempsey Nordhaus, an English instructor at Gateway Technical College in Wisconsin, is a writing center specialist at the College of Lake County in Illinois. She first became interested in writing centers while completing her MA in writing at DePaul University. Her other interests include developmental writing, business communication, and creative nonfiction.

Ben Rafoth directs the writing center and teaches undergraduate and graduate courses at Indiana University of Pennsylvania in Indiana, Pennsylvania. He has published articles in various composition journals and is the editor of *A Tutor's Guide: Helping Writers One to One* (Boynton/Cook, 2000).

Carol Severino is Associate Professor of Rhetoric and Director of the writing center at the University of Iowa, where she has recently helped to construct and direct a Writing Fellows (peer tutoring/writing across the curriculum) program. She researches and teaches about how culture and language background influence writing and writing pedagogy and serves on the editorial boards of the *Journal of Second Language Writing*, *College Composition and Communication*, and *Writing Center Journal*.

Jennifer Staben is an English instructor and writing center coordinator at the College of Lake County in Illinois. She had her first tutoring experiences as a graduate student at the University of Iowa. Her research interests include writing centers, literacy, and ESL writers.

Theresa Jiinling Tseng is a PhD candidate in Composition and TESOL at Indiana University of Pennsylvania (IUP). She has taught ESL, EFL, as well as English teacher training courses for 17 years and has co-authored three English writing textbooks, *Writing Practice Book I, II and III* (San Min/Dong Da).

Author Index

Subject Index